Conversations with Michael Chabon

Literary Conversations Series

Conversations
with Michael Chabon

Edited by Brannon Costello

University Press of Mississippi   Jackson

Books by Michael Chabon
The Mysteries of Pittsburgh. New York: William Morrow, 1988.
A Model World and Other Stories. New York: William Morrow, 1991.
Wonder Boys. New York: Villard, 1995.
Werewolves in Their Youth. New York: Random House, 1999.
The Amazing Adventures of Kavalier & Clay. New York: Random House, 2000.
Summerland. New York: Miramax, 2002.
The Final Solution: A Story of Detection. New York: HarperCollins, 2004.
Gentlemen of the Road. New York: Del Rey, 2007.
The Yiddish Policemen's Union. New York: HarperCollins, 2007.
Maps and Legends. San Francisco: McSweeney's, 2008.
Manhood for Amateurs: The Pleasures and Regrets of a Husband, Father, and Son. New York: HarperCollins, 2009.
The Astonishing Secret of Awesome Man (with illustrator Jake Parker). New York: Balzer & Bray, 2011.
Telegraph Avenue. New York: HarperCollins, 2012.

Edited Collections
McSweeney's Mammoth Treasury of Thrilling Tales. New York: Vintage, 2003.
McSweeney's Enchanted Chamber of Astonishing Stories. New York: Vintage, 2004.
The Best American Short Stories. New York: Houghton Mifflin, 2005.

www.upress.state.ms.us

The University Press of Mississippi is a member
    of the Association of American University Presses.
Copyright © 2015 by University Press of Mississippi
All rights reserved
Manufactured in the United States of America
First printing 2015
∞

Library of Congress Cataloging-in-Publication Data

Chabon, Michael.
  Conversations with Michael Chabon / edited by Brannon Costello.
      pages cm. — (Literary conversations series)
  Includes index.
    ISBN 978-1-62846-233-3 (hardback) — ISBN 978-1-62674-669-5 (ebook) 1. Chabon, Michael—Interviews. 2. Novelists, American—20th century—Interviews. 3. Fiction—Authorship. I. Costello, Brannon, 1975– editor. II. Title.
  PS3553.H15Z46 2015
  813'.54—dc23
  [B]   2014039246
British Library Cataloging-in-Publication Data available

Contents

Introduction

In a 2000 interview with Michael Silverblatt, Michael Chabon cut to the essence of his writerly ambitions. He remarked, "[M]y only goal, ever, really, is to try to write the kind of book that I think I would like to read—and I read for pleasure."[1] Even a cursory glance at his novels, short story collections, and essays reveals the depth and breadth of those pleasures—everything from harrowing tales of supernatural adventure to contemplative stories of everyday epiphanies. Given the critical acclaim and commercial success his work has enjoyed, it's clear that the reading public has found many of Chabon's pleasures to be its own. But the true measure of his influence in contemporary literature might be best reflected in cartoonist Daniel Clowes's cover illustration for the *New Yorker*'s June 4/11, 2012 issue. Titled "Crashing the Gate," it depicts a stereotypical cocktail party for the cultural intelligentsia in a moment of sudden crisis. A tear has opened in the fabric of reality, tossing the host's well-stocked bookshelves into disarray and admitting a strange and garish assemblage of otherworldly creatures: a green-tentacled alien, a retro-futuristic robot, and a heavily pomaded spaceman. The image is an apt introduction for the venerable magazine's first-ever "Science Fiction Issue." In its pages, stories and essays by acknowledged masters of science fiction and fantasy such as Ray Bradbury, Ursula K. Le Guin, and China Miéville appear alongside pieces by writers of so-called literary fiction such as Jennifer Egan, Junot Diaz, and Colson Whitehead. Though the bespectacled, drably attired party guests of the issue's cover react to the newcomers' arrival with shock and dismay, the issue's contents tell a different story: one of conviviality and collaboration, one in which authors once considered part of marginal genres are hailed as major voices in contemporary literature and writers from the literary mainstream engage with speculative fiction in a deep and complex way.

It is difficult to imagine this state of affairs coming to pass without the efforts of Michael Chabon. Chabon's relentless advocacy on behalf of genres frequently dismissed as subliterary pulp entertainments—not to mention the heap of accolades his own genre-bending work has accumulated—has helped create a literary marketplace in which the fantastic and the quotidian can sit comfortably together on the same bookshelf, or even between the covers of a single book. Indeed, in the pages of that *New Yorker* issue, Le Guin describes Chabon as an ally of Clowes's interlopers. Chabon, she writes, "came crashing like a golem out of Berkeley across the genre walls and through the gated communities and left them in rubble."[2] Chabon is not, of course, the first writer to find a way through the wall between literary and pulp fiction. Rick Moody's *The Ice Storm* (1994) used Stan Lee and Jack Kirby's *Fantastic Four* comics to reflect on the sublimely complicated nature of family life, and Jack Butler's *Jujitsu for Christ* (1986) drew upon superhero comics and science fiction novels to express the intensity and strangeness of growing up in the heat and violence of 1960s Mississippi—to name only a couple of examples. And I don't mean to elide the distinctive approaches to popular genres that writers such as Egan, Diaz, and Whitehead have individually developed. But the widespread praise for *The Amazing Adventures of Kavalier & Clay* (2000), with its buoyant enthusiasm for the mad dreamers and frustrated artists laboring in the treacherous commercial underworld of Golden Age comic books, made Chabon something of an unofficial diplomat tasked with brokering peaceful relations between the tweedy aesthetes and the otherworldly invaders of Clowes's cover.

As these interviews reveal, from Chabon's perspective, such a mission has less to do with finding common ground between two fundamentally alien civilizations than it does with excavating the history of a once capacious and diverse literary homeland that has been arbitrarily hacked up into a jumble of multiple, sometimes warring, nations. In a 2003 interview with Neil Gaiman, Chabon recounts how his growing dissatisfaction with the limited scope of the contemporary short story led him to examine his library of classic short story anthologies. Chabon explains,

> [L]ooking through them I noticed two things right away. A lot of them were what we would now call genre stories: ghost stories, western stories, war stories, horror stories, suspense stories. Then I noticed that a lot of these genre stories were written by people like Edith Wharton, Henry James, Joseph Conrad, and Somerset Maugham. Apparently, there didn't used to be as strict a ghettoization of the genres of literature as there is now. And maybe because of that, writers whom we now consider to be serious literary writers were free to write in any genre they felt like.

He continues, "There's a whole set of tools we're not using." Seen from Chabon's perspective, then, Clowes's image perhaps depicts not the initial meeting between two alien cultures but, rather, a sort of homecoming—a reunification after a period of regrettable partition. Chabon's rediscovery of the power of the works that ignited his youthful love of fiction and his growing conviction that there is nothing inherently unserious about so-called genre work are recurring themes in the interviews collected here. These concerns often overlap and intersect with other frequently discussed themes, as Chabon's reading life is densely imbricated with other aspects of his personal and intellectual life, including his relationship to his Jewish heritage, the fluidity of sexual identity, the difficulties and rewards of family life, the mythology and iconography of America, and the development of his own distinctive voice.

Unlike most authors, Chabon began his career in the bright glare of the spotlight. Even before his debut novel, *The Mysteries of Pittsburgh* (1988), appeared on the shelves, the literary world was a-chatter with the story behind its publication: a professor in his MFA program secretly submitted the manuscript to a literary agent, who helped secure Chabon a sizable advance rare for a first-time author. Chabon's earliest interviews, then, were short profiles from major national newspapers that highlight his status as the next big thing. Chabon's 1988 interview with Helen Dudar of the *Wall Street Journal* is a good example of the genre, focusing primarily on his youth and sudden celebrity and addressing his bemusement at being (as he puts it) "mispigeonholed" as a gay writer because the novel's male protagonist has a love affair with a man.[3] Though these early pieces are of some historical interest, I have not included any full interviews from this era. Instead, I've opted to emphasize the more substantial interviews that began to appear slightly later in his career.

After the publication of his first short story collection, *A Model World and Other Stories*, Chabon withdrew from the public eye somewhat as he struggled to complete the intended follow-up to *The Mysteries of Pittsburgh*, the sprawling and eventually abandoned novel called *Fountain City*. Chabon often reflects upon the trials endured and the lessons learned during this difficult period, particularly when the conversation turns to the novel that Chabon ultimately finished instead, *Wonder Boys*. The protagonist of that novel, Grady Tripp, is striving to conquer a steadily metastasizing novel of his own and must, like Chabon, learn to let it go. It is perhaps no accident that *Wonder Boys* begins with Chabon's most explicit engagement with the fiction of fantasy and adventure that would animate so much of his subsequent output: an invocation of the fictional pulp writer August Van Zorn (aka Albert Vetch), an obscure master of the "weird tale" genre. Van Zorn's macabre stories and tragic suicide haunt Grady's life, but writing about Van Zorn and his milieu clearly energized Chabon's work.

Several of the stories in *Werewolves in Their Youth* (1999), Chabon's second short story collection, continue to chart Chabon's explorations of the hidden depths of popular culture and genre fiction. Of particular note is "In the Black Mill," a Lovecraftian horror story written in Van Zorn's voice. As Chabon reflects ruefully in a 2012 interview with David Barr Kirtley and John Joseph Adams, he first submitted that story to the *New Yorker*, where "it spent a very brief period of time on the editorial desk . . . before reemerging with its dignity somewhat in tatters." "In the Black Mill" eventually appeared in *Playboy*, but the *New Yorker*'s quick refusal of a "genre" story— and one by a writer whose more conventionally literary stories had often been featured in the magazine's pages before—suggests the stubbornness of the prejudices against such approaches to fiction at the most prestigious literary outlets. The success of Chabon's next novel would demonstrate the limitations of such orthodoxies of literary value. *The Amazing Adventures of Kavalier & Clay* was a popular success and earned Chabon a Pulitzer Prize, so it's no surprise that Chabon maintained his enthusiastic and thoughtful investigation of putatively trashy genres in the works to follow. In addition to tracking his history as a reader in the essays eventually collected in *Maps and Legends* (2008), Chabon edited a special issue of *McSweeney's* dedicated to scuffing the chalk line between literary and lowbrow; its contributors included everyone from Stephen King to Rick Moody. Chabon also published a young-adult adventure novel, *Summerland* (2002), a sprawling yarn that wove together baseball, Norse mythology, and Native American trickster stories. *Summerland* was followed by *The Final Solution* (2004), a short novel that paid homage to the shaping influence of the Sherlock Holmes stories of Sir Arthur Conan Doyle—the author who first inspired Chabon to put pen to paper.

Chabon's next works not only reflected his continued interest in grand adventure but also his deeper explorations of Jewish culture. Indeed, the two are closely connected: in a 2008 interview with *Locus*, he remarks, "I came to realize recently that as I was going through [the process of] turning my back on being Jewish and then, in a sense, rediscovering it and reincorporating it into my life—that process almost exactly paralleled what happened to me with science fiction, fantasy, and detective mystery fiction as well." In a 1996 interview with Bob Goodman, Chabon recalls being stung early in his career by Cynthia Ozick's dismissive appraisal: "He may be Jewish and he may be a writer, but he's not a Jewish writer." Though her judgment was off-base, Chabon muses, "I realized that before I could have someone like Cynthia Ozick judge me differently, I would have to establish to myself to what degree I was a Jewish writer. I had just taken it for granted, and I was forced to think about it. I'll probably go on wrestling with it for some time. I've joined the eternal debate over who is a Jew." The fruits of Chabon's participation in this debate are evident in *Gentlemen of the Road* (2007). A swashbuckling sword-and-sorcery adventure in the tradition of Fritz Leiber and Robert E. Howard, *Gentlemen* takes place in a now all-but-forgotten ancient Jewish kingdom. The same year, Chabon published *The Yiddish Policemen's Union*, a crime novel inspired by Raymond Chandler and Dashiell Hammett set in an alternate history where displaced European Jews settled in Alaska after World War II. *The Yiddish Policemen's Union* not only won acclaim from mainstream literary outlets but also received the Hugo and Nebula Awards, the most coveted prizes in science fiction. Even *Manhood for Amateurs: The Pleasures and Regrets of a Husband, Father, and Son* (2009), his second nonfiction collection, combined Chabon's love for space opera and superhero comics with his reflections on Jewish identity, as when he uses the writings of Edgar Rice Burroughs to think through the issues around the choice to circumcise his son. Chabon's most recent novel, *Telegraph Avenue* (2012), drew inspiration from his childhood in the integrated community of Columbia, Maryland, for its treatment of the complex relationship between Jewish and African American culture. In 2013, Chabon described this relationship to me as a "hall of mirrors in which blacks and Jews have lived in American culture, where they're endlessly reflecting each other and being in turn reflected back again." Given its contemporary California setting, many critics characterized *Telegraph Avenue* as a return to realism, and reasonably enough. But its loving attention to Blaxploitation and martial arts movies, the writings of H. P. Lovecraft, and conspiracy theories underscores an essential truth of Chabon's fiction: that our fantasies and our reality are so tightly woven together as to be inextricable.

Though this very brief sketch of Chabon's career emphasizes the fiction writing for which he is best known, Chabon speaks thoughtfully and candidly about his work in other genres and mediums in these interviews. He has written for comics, including material featuring his own creations from *The Amazing Adventures of Kavalier & Clay* for the Dark Horse Comics series *The Amazing Adventures of The Escapist* as well as stories for DC Comics' *JSA All-Stars* and for the forthcoming volume of Matt Fraction, Gabriel Ba, and Fabio Moon's *Casanova*. Chabon has also written for the screen, including contributions to *Spider-Man 2* and *John Carter*. His enthusiasm for helping to bring the icons of his childhood to the silver screen is evident in these pieces. But such work is fraught with peril as well, and Chabon also discusses the difficulties entailed in the collaborative, heavily managed process of screenwriting, in which the writer's vision is necessarily beholden to a vast and unknowable legion of producers, financiers, and studio executives.

Such constraints are antithetical to Chabon's pursuit of his own singular vision in fiction, and these interviews provide valuable insights into his practical writing methods and strategies and the philosophies that undergird them. The interplay between the mystery of inspiration and the hard work of shoe-leather (or mouse pad) research—whether it's reading old WPA guides, plunging into the history of Yiddish, interviewing veteran comic book artists, or investigating the world of midwifery—is a subject of particular interest to Chabon. As he notes in a 2000 interview with Barbara Shoup and Margaret-Love Denman, research has its seductive pleasures. But, he claims, "doing too much research sometimes started to make me feel imprisoned by the facts. There always comes a point when you have to put research aside and start making stuff up." Though he insists on the importance of maintaining a regular writing schedule, he also admits to eschewing intensive planning. While Chabon acknowledges that this approach can sometimes be costly, it is perhaps appropriate for a writer who does not privilege plot above other aspects of fiction. Indeed, in a 2000 interview with Michael Silverblatt, Chabon even likens the act of writing fiction to the escape artistry of Harry Houdini: he describes plot as "this horrible, nightmarish contraption [that] you begin to fasten . . . around yourself," with the novel itself a kind of record of the author's escape from it. Though Chabon acknowledges the difficulty of weaving together plot, theme, and character into a convincing whole, a bright thread running throughout these interviews is his conviction that the core of his approach to writing is the richness of language itself—the possibility that a well-turned phrase can unlock a new perception of the world.

The interviews in this volume are reprinted as they originally appeared, though some minor errors have been silently corrected. They are organized chronologically in the order in which they were conducted (rather than published), to the extent that this information could be determined. As befits a writer as prolific and multifaceted as Michael Chabon, the interviews collected here come from a wide variety of sources, including literary journals, science fiction magazines, pop-culture podcasts, and general-interest online venues. One benefit of this diversity is that each interview tends to approach Chabon's work with a unique set of concerns and assumptions; thus, there is little repetition across the interviews. Nevertheless, some repetition is inevitable—and indeed, the repetition itself can be revealing, as one of Chabon's strengths as an interview subject is his ability to find an illuminating new angle on even an oft-told story.

I was fortunate to benefit from the generosity and diligence of many people when compiling the materials for this volume. I owe a particular debt of gratitude to my graduate research assistants Matt Dischinger and Amy Rossi, who more than capably acquitted themselves as ace transcriptionists, keen-eyed proofreaders, and thorough researchers. Many thanks are also due Amy Cray, Michael Chabon's supremely efficient and helpful assistant, who responded to my endless queries with patience and insight. Working with the University Press of Mississippi has been, as always, a pleasure. In particular, I owe thanks to Walter Biggins, who originally approved this project, for his enthusiasm and encouragement; to Katie Keene, who has shepherded it to completion, for her wisdom and expertise; and to Shane Gong and Anne Stascavage for the painstaking work of transforming the manuscript into the book you now hold. Along the way I have been assisted by a host of kind souls who have offered feedback, tracked down contacts for permissions, looked for copies of hard-to-find magazines, and generally greased the many and various wheels that needed turning: to Matt Fraction, Cat Mihos, Sarah Nagel, Michael Silverblatt, and my faithful writing partner Sue Weinstein, I offer my heartfelt appreciation. It goes without saying that none of my projects would get off the ground without the support and encouragement of Gina Costello, but I will say it anyway. Finally, particular thanks to Michael Chabon for consenting to the final interview, for reviewing the chronology, and for giving so generously of his time and assistance in putting this volume together.

BC

Notes

1. Unless otherwise noted, all interviews cited are included in this volume.

2. Ursula K. Le Guin, "The Golden Age." *New Yorker* 4/11 June 2012: 77.

3. Helen Dudar, "Instant Fame for a First Novelist." *Wall Street Journal* 10 May 1988. *Factiva*. Web. 20 May 2013.

Chronology

1989   Chabon publishes three short stories: "More Than Human" appears in *Gentleman's Quarterly*, and "A Model World" and "Ocean Avenue" appear in the *New Yorker*.

1990   Four more of Chabon's stories appear the *New Yorker*: "The Lost World," "Millionaires," "S ANGEL," and "Smoke."

1991   Chabon releases a collection of short stories entitled *A Model World and Other Stories*. He and Groth divorce.

1992   Chabon publishes the short story "Mrs. Box" in the *New Yorker*.

1993   Chabon marries lawyer (and future novelist) Ayelet Waldman. Chabon also publishes the short story "Werewolves in Their Youth" in the *New Yorker*. After abandoning *Fountain City*, he begins work on *Wonder Boys*.

1994   Chabon publishes the short story "House Hunting" in the *New Yorker*. His screenplay *The Gentleman Host* is optioned by producer Scott Rudin but never produced. Chabon and Waldman's first child, Sophie, is born.

1995   Chabon publishes his long-awaited second novel, *Wonder Boys*, and begins work on *The Amazing Adventures of Kavalier & Clay*. Chabon also works up a film proposal, unused, for a *Fantastic Four* movie.

1996   Chabon prepares a script treatment, ultimately unused, for the first *X-Men* film.

1997   Chabon and Waldman settle in Berkeley, California. Their second child, Ezekiel, is born. Chabon publishes three short stories: "That Was Me" in the *New Yorker*, "The Harris Fetko Story" in *Esquire*, and "In the Black Mill" in *Playboy*. Chabon also publishes the essay "Guidebook to a Land of Ghosts" in *Civilization* (later reprinted in *Harper's* as "The Language of Lost History").

1998   Chabon publishes the short story "Son of the Wolfman" in *Harper's*.

1999   Chabon releases his second collection of short stories, *Werewolves in Their Youth*. A portions of Chabon's novel in progress, *The Amazing Adventures of Kavalier & Clay*, is released in the *New Yorker* as "The Hofzinser Club." The *New Yorker* names Chabon one of the best fiction writers under forty. Chabon writes an unproduced television pilot for CBS entitled "House of Gold" and begins work on the television pilot that will eventually evolve into the novel *Telegraph Avenue*.

2000   The film *Wonder Boys*, based on Chabon's novel of the same name, is released in February. In September, Random House publishes *The Amazing Adventures of Kavalier & Clay*. Chabon begins work on the young-adult novel *Summerland*.

2001   Chabon wins the Pulitzer Prize for Fiction for *The Amazing Adventures of Kavalier & Clay*. His stories "The God of Dark Laughter" and "Along the Frontage Road" appear in the *New Yorker*. "The Return of the Amazing Cavalieri: From Untold Tales of Kavalier & Clay" appears in *McSweeney's*. Chabon begins work on *The Final Solution*. Chabon and Waldman's third child, Ida-Rose, is born.

2002   Miramax publishes Chabon's young-adult novel *Summerland. McSweeney's* publishes its Chabon-edited tenth issue, *McSweeney's Mammoth Treasury of Thrilling Tales*, a wide-ranging collection of genre fiction with illustrations by cartoonist Howard Chaykin. Chabon releases the first chapter of *Fountain City*, his unpublished novel, and an unproduced television script entitled "Garageland" on his website.

2003   Chabon's fourth child, Abraham, is born. Chabon begins work on *The Yiddish Policemen's Union*. Vintage releases a mass-market paperback edition of *McSweeney's* #10. His story "The Final Solution: A Story of Detection" appears in the *Paris Review*. Chabon's story "The Strange Case of Mr. Terrific and Doctor Nil" appears in DC Comics' *JSA All-Stars* #7 with art by Michael Lark. *Summerland* receives the Mythopoeic Fantasy Award.

2004   *The Final Solution* and the Chabon-edited *McSweeney's Enchanted Chamber of Astonishing Stories* are published. Dark Horse Comics begins publishing *The Amazing Adventures of The Escapist*, a comics anthology featuring characters from *The Amazing Adventures of Kavalier & Clay. Virginia Quarterly Review* publishes "The Origin of the Escapist" later that year along with "An Untold Tale of Kavalier & Clay: Breakfast in the Wreck." In July, Chabon delivers the keynote speech at the Eisner Awards at Comic-Con International in San Diego. The film *Spider-Man 2*, to which Chabon contributed script work, is released.

2005   Publication of *The Amazing Adventures of the Escapist* continues, including a full-length story written by Chabon in issue 7. Chabon also edits and writes the introduction for *The Best American Short Stories 2005*. Chabon begins what would become a monthly column for *Details*. Many of those columns would later be republished in Chabon's essay collection *Manhood for Amateurs. The Amazing*

Conversations with Michael Chabon

Michael Chabon:
Wonder Boy in Transition

Lisa See Kendall / 1995

From *Publishers Weekly* 10 April 1995. © *Publishers Weekly*. Reprinted by permission.

Michael Chabon, once pegged as a wonder boy for his first novel, *The Mysteries of Pittsburgh*, languidly lounges in an overstuffed chair in his Spanish duplex in Los Angeles. With lanky hair, loose-fitting clothes, and a modest demeanor, he looks like a nice boy that any mother would be happy to see her daughter bring home. He's self-deprecating, soft-spoken, and he has the endearing habit of paying more attention to the squeals of delight issuing from his four-month-old daughter in the back bedroom than to the discussion of his long-anticipated new novel, *Wonder Boys*, just released by Villard. The novel has wonderfully wry connotations. Narrator Grady Tripp, once deemed a "wonder boy" on the strength of his first novel, remains mired in his second attempt, a hopelessly long work-in-progress called *Wonder Boys*. His editor, Terry Crabtee, also once a rising star, is on the skids. And the next generation is coming up fast: at the college where Grady teaches, a talented but incurably mendacious student seems poised to begin a stellar writing career.

Chabon knows whereof he speaks. His own career took off like a rocket, and then slumped into a waiting game. Born in 1963 in Washington, DC, and raised in Columbia, Maryland, Chabon recalls that he had a love of words from early childhood. "I liked word etymologies," he says. "I was always a good speller. I guess that my love of language is chiefly a function of having a good memory for words, like having an ear for music. My parents were big readers and my grandmother used to read poetry to me."

Pittsburgh has also been a major influence in his life. After a year at Carnegie Mellon, he transferred to the University of Pittsburgh, where he graduated with a B.A. in English in 1984. Then he crossed the country to the University of California at Irvine, where he entered the M.F.A. program run by Oakley Hall and Donald Heiney, who wrote under the name MacDonald Harris.

Heartened when he won a *Mademoiselle* short story contest in 1987, Chabon wrote *The Mysteries of Pittsburgh* for his master's thesis. He turned in the final draft on a Friday. The following Monday Chabon found a note in his box from Heiney/Harris, saying that he had sent the manuscript to agent Mary Evans at the Virginia Barber Agency in New York. Two months later, Evans sold the book to editor Doug Stumpf at Morrow.

Published in 1988, *The Mysteries of Pittsburgh* made a major splash, garnering a spot on the *Publishers Weekly* bestseller list for seven weeks. Chabon was instantly lumped with other brat packers of the day—Jay McInerney, Tama Janowitz and Bret Easton Ellis. The Gap asked him to model jeans; he turned down the offer.

People magazine wanted to include him in its "50 Most Beautiful People" issue; he turned that down, too. Looking back, Chabon says he wishes he'd appreciated that time more for the "amazing ride" that it was. "But I was married at that point to a would-be writer. The fact that nothing like this was happening to her made it difficult for me to enjoy what was happening. All the good things were a mixed blessing." Nor did he particularly care for being identified with the brat pack. "I never thought I had anything in common with the usual suspects; but I suppose that 'youth' was the main handle, an inevitable handle. I just didn't pay much attention to it. I was twenty-three. I thought in terms of what did I have in common with Cheever, Nabokov, or Flaubert when they were twenty-three? I had high aims."

Chabon says he strived very hard not to be the flavor-of-the-month or a cool member of the New York literati scene, but instead to refine his craft. He worked on short stories, many of which were published in the *New Yorker* and *GQ*. He also wrote travel articles—on Key West, Prague, Las Vegas, and Tuscany—for *Vogue* and the *New York Times*. By 1991, when his collection of short stories, *A Model World*, was released, Chabon was already two years into his second novel, a sprawling saga called *Fountain City*, that was gradually becoming his albatross.

Coming up with a second novel is hard for any writer. For Chabon, there was the intense pressure of having to produce something that would meet and surpass the promise of *Mysteries*. The plot of *Fountain City* involved Paris and Florida, utopian dreamers and ecological activists, architecture and baseball, an Israeli spy and a man dying from AIDS, a love affair between a young American and a woman ten years his senior.

An Incompetent Handyman

As he struggled for five years to make the Paris half of the book mesh with the Florida half, his personal life was in constant flux. He moved six times. He got divorced from his first wife, took up with another woman, split up, met Ayelet Waldman, and married her. All the while, the unfinished book was almost a palpable burden. "You know that scene at the Seder in *Wonder Boys* when someone asks Grady how his book is going? I can't tell you how many times I was asked that. I always felt like an incompetent handyman. I always thought that I was just about done." Instead, it was never done. "Doug Stumpf kept saying that it was full of amazing stuff. I'd try to fix it, cut it, restructure it." Chabon estimates that he wrote 1,500 pages of what he tried to turn into a 700-page—and still unpublishable—manuscript.

At the beginning of 1993, Chabon and Waldman, who was clerking for a federal judge, lived in San Francisco. She was due to take the bar exam in July. Instead, she decided to tackle it earlier, in February, which meant that she would be studying nonstop for the following six weeks. After her announcement, Chabon went downstairs to his basement office, turned on the computer and fantasized longingly—as he had done every day for years—about the book he would rather be writing.

He imagined a scene: a troubled young man standing in a backyard, holding a derringer to his temple, while, on a nearby porch, a shaggy, pot-smoking, older man tries to decide if what he's seeing is real or not. Chabon elected to pursue the idea. He wrote fifteen pages in the first four hours, producing what eventually became a pivotal scene in *Wonder Boys*. "It was flowing out in a way that I remembered from *Mysteries of Pittsburgh*," he recalls. By the end of the first day, he also knew that the story would take place in Pittsburgh.

"After *Mysteries*, I never intended to use that city again in my writing," he says. "I don't really have an explanation for my fascination with the place, except perhaps that my father moved there when I was twelve. I spent my summers and holidays there. And, of course, I attended college there. Pittsburgh is where I became who I am now. College formed my ideas on art, literature, friends, sex. It's where I started to write in earnest." Just as in *Mysteries*, the new project—which Chabon stored in his computer simply as X—was written in the first person. "I like to read books that are in the first person. I like the intimate confessional tone, as though the person has pulled up a chair and is telling you about his life."

Revising a Life

Chabon kept X a secret. Within a matter of days, he'd written fifty pages of what became an intricate plot. In addition to his endlessly revised manuscript, Grady Tripp is—in ways that he cannot control—revising his life. He loves his wife and everyone in her family, but he's having an affair with the wife of the chairman of the English department. His dissolute editor is trying to wrest the manuscript from Tripp to salvage his own career. But what drives this wacky, almost slapstick, tale are the subplots. They involve a tuba, a dead dog, a dead boa constrictor, the fur-trimmed satin jacket worn by Marilyn Monroe at her wedding to Joe DiMaggio, and that hefty manuscript.

Six weeks later, after his wife took the bar exam, he gave her the first 117 pages to read and was amazed at her reaction. Incredibly, he hadn't thought of the book as humorous. "I'm not at all an intentional writer," Chabon concedes. "I don't plan. I don't think about how my writing will strike the reader. To me, Grady has a wry tone, but I felt sad writing about him. In a lot of ways, he is a projection of my worst fears of what I was going to become if I kept working on *Fountain City*. So it wasn't until Ayelet read the manuscript that I realized it was funny."

Having completed the first draft in seven months, he called Mary Evans with the good news that he'd finally finished his second novel, but that it wasn't *Fountain City*. Fortunately, his contract with Villard was simply for a novel.

Nevertheless, the road to publication was bumpy. Over an eight-month span, Chabon's agent and editor played musical chairs. Mary Evans left the Virginia Barber agency and went out on her own. Doug Stumpf, who edited the book, then exited Villard for *Vanity Fair*, leaving publisher David Rosenthal to shepherd the novel. At the same time, Villard's publicity department was undergoing an upheaval. Mary Evans persuaded Villard to hire independent publicist Susan Ostrov to give the book the special attention it deserved. On a personal level, Chabon moved once again when Waldman took a job in Los Angeles as a federal public defender. And Sophie was born.

A letter from Stumpf accompanies the galleys of *Wonder Boys*. Stumpf writes that the theme of the book is "the terrible emotional and spiritual cost of not growing up." Chabon, who does not know about the letter until *PW* mentions it, is somewhat bemused. He's never really understood the idea of themes in novels, he says, and continues: "To me, the book is about the disappointment of getting older and growing up and not measuring up to what you thought, and the world and the people in it not being what you expected. It's about disillusionment and acceptance."

Chabon has drawn two lessons from his failure to complete *Fountain City* and the ease and joy of writing *Wonder Boys*. "Don't take advances on books, because they put too much pressure on you," he advises. "And don't be afraid to abandon something you don't like." Another lesson might be that when the words start to sing, follow them.

So far, *Wonder Boys* seems to be singing a happy tune. Villard is sending Chabon on a nine-city tour; audio rights have been sold to Brilliance; and Avon has a substantial floor for the paperback. Steve Rubin (producer of *The Firm*) has optioned the book for Paramount. Rubin also optioned *The Gentleman Host*, an original screenplay that Chabon wrote for fast cash when Waldman announced she was pregnant. The story concerns the so-called gentlemen hosts who, in exchange for free trips, agree to dance and play cards with women on cruise ships. "In retrospect, it wasn't the most commercial idea," says Chabon. "But I feel close to the older generation of Jews, people in their seventies and eighties. I was very close to my grandfather, who died about six years ago. I have felt his absence and have looked for ways to fill the gap." Chabon may be the only successful writer who also does volunteer work in an old-age home.

The publishing world is littered with former wonder boys, but every once in a while a young writer comes along who goes on to fulfill his early promise. *Wonder Boys* may indeed be the means by which Chabon becomes one of the few *wunderkinds* of his generation who makes the transition to a mature writer with a solid future. Maybe now he'll be able to enjoy his amazing ride.

Michael Chabon

Michael Silverblatt / 1995

From *Bookworm*. KCRW, Santa Monica, CA, 29 May 1995. Web. © KCRW *Bookworm*. http://
www.kcrw.com/etc/programs/bw. Reprinted by permission. Michael Silverblatt is the
coproducer and host of KCRW's *Bookworm*.

Michael Silverblatt: Welcome to *Bookworm*. My guest is Michael Chabon, the author most recently of *Wonder Boys*, published by Villard Books. Michael, surely everyone must have been afraid of a book that was going to be about a writer and his editor and a writing workshop, however farcical and hilarious it turned out to be. Were you cautioned?

Michael Chabon: No, I wasn't, but only because nobody knew I was writing it until they actually had it in their hands. I had been writing another book for many years, and finally, after a lot of pain and emotional turmoil, I decided to dump it, and I started writing this book. But I didn't tell anyone I had done it, including my wife. I just started it and had about 110 pages after six weeks, at which point I did tell my wife but not anyone else. So nobody saw it until the first draft was done, and by then it was too late to warn me.

Silverblatt: Were you afraid?

Chabon: A little bit at first—after I had about fifteen pages and I realized, oh my god I'm writing a book about a writer. Then two things happened. One is, although I understand there seems to be a kind of prejudice against books by writers about writers, personally it's a genre that I've always really liked. Some of my favorite books [are about that topic]—*The Ghost Writer*, the Frederick Exley book *A Fan's Notes*—and it's something I always enjoy reading. So I told myself, well don't worry about it, it'll be okay. Then the second thing was just that I was enjoying it so much that I stopped worrying, because I figured if I was enjoying it then other people would too.

8

Silverblatt: It turned into a comedy. Most of those books, like *A Fan's Notes*, are books out of which self-recognition comes out of despair, and although the hero-narrator of this book does come to a self-recognition in its final pages, the reader's experience is one of high farce, so that it reads more like Moliere making fun of the doctors and hypocrites of his world than like an angst-ridden and soul-baring novel.

Chabon: Well, good! I'm glad of that [*laughter*].

Silverblatt: I was talking last night with Susan Sontag, and she was telling me that she was, of all things, rereading J. D. Salinger, and that she couldn't imagine enjoying a book about Princeton students dating one another and meeting after the big game but that the writing was so deft and pleasurable and struck so many stray and arbitrary and pleasant postures that you can't get enough of it. And that's always what I've taken to be the quality of your writing as well—that the writing is brandishing so many writing strategies, it's doing so much, that it hardly matters what the subject is. The language seems to be going over the falls in a barrel.

Chabon: Well, thank you very much. I guess I rely on that to keep me from having to worry too much about the fact that maybe I don't have the most radical ideas of social philosophy to dispense through my writing, or [tales of] my travels in the Yucatan and to the top of Mount Kilimanjaro and things like that. Every so often maybe I have a moment's pause and think, is this really something somebody's going to want to read about? I try to reassure myself, I tell myself I just have to make it sound good enough and that will hopefully please the reader.

Silverblatt: I remember I met you once at a writer's conference and we saw standing by a ski mountainside some child looking importunate, sort of like a Dickensian orphan, and you started to do a riff about the child begging for ice lollies, and I thought, oh, what a good word to have suddenly graced her with. That's to say that the style of your writing seems to be full of pastiche— words come in from everywhere, from all sorts of literary sources. I think about hearing in Nabokov certain kinds of pairings of adjectives. It seems like you work first on style before anything else.

Chabon: Well, I work on it, and yet I've always been very porous to language. From my earliest memories, I've always been interested in words and in etymologies and in vocabulary lists and in derivations and word histories, and I think there's something about the way my brain is set up that I don't necessarily have to work on a sentence to get it to come out sounding the way I want it to. I often find that it's more a question of hearing a kind of idealized rhythm of a sentence in my mind just moments before I know I'm going to need it, and then once I need it it's there in some strange way, as if I just reach out my hand to it. I mean, I will go over my writing over and over and over again trying to get the sound right, but at some level it's very much an unconscious kind of thing that arises in some way out of my love of language, in particular of English.

Silverblatt: It's interesting, because I began to think you've been praised for all of these books in particular because of the ability for the book to describe a state of mind without falling into it, without participating in it or bathing in it—*bathos* is not a primary quality of your writing. The first novel, *The Mysteries of Pittsburgh*, is about the finding of sexual identity; the second one seems to be about the dissolution of families, families falling apart, and narrators who are rather badly buffeted by this kind of dishevelment; and the third one, *Wonder Boys*, is a book more or less about writer's block and what kinds of extravaganzas of life-invention come up at that moment when the creation is no longer going on meaningfully on the page. So I began to think that you have this way of dealing with some of the most traumatizing things for writers to go through, for anyone to go through, but because of the facility with language, it becomes an adventure rather than a catastrophe.

Chabon: Well, my favorite writers tend to be in some measure ironists, like Nabokov or John Cheever. S. J. Perelman is a great favorite of mine. One of the things I've learned from them is to always maintain a certain distance from the sufferings of your characters, that it's healthy, and it actually produces more of an emotional response in the reader if they can stand at a certain remove from a character than if you sort of just shove them face-first into the emotional turmoil—although there are plenty of writers who are extremely good at doing just that and producing very moving pieces of fiction. But if it is true that I can avoid, say, *bathos*, that's because I'm always trying to introduce notes of self-mockery. Grady in *Wonder Boys* is very self-mocking, and any time he begins to verge into self-pity he immediately gives himself kind of a sharp slap across the face and tells himself that that's just what he's doing.

Silverblatt: People criticize Perelman for what seems to them like a cellophane sound of language crackling with no interiors, and although I definitely do not feel this way, there are people who always felt Nabokov to be elitist and cold. What's interesting here about that kind of distance is that everyone seems to get—and this is why I think of Salinger or the early Capote—a bit of charitableness, a kind of kindness or tenderness expended on them that you don't usually think of as a quality of ironic writing.

Chabon: I hope that's the case. For the most part the characters in my books, no matter what the state of their relations with each other, have a kind of affection for one another. I've noticed that my characters are often expressing sudden bursts of affection for random people, characters who intrude into the book for a paragraph and then disappear. There's a bus driver in *The Mysteries of Pittsburgh* who is the beneficiary of a little eulogy from the narrator even though he appears for less than a paragraph. I don't know where that comes from exactly, but I think that, in tandem with trying to maintain my distance from the characters or keep the readers just a little bit removed from them, within the story the characters themselves are very much attached to one another, and maybe that produces the kind of thing you're talking about.

Silverblatt: In all of the books there are certain kind of leitmotif images that don't exactly become symbolic, like the cloud factory in *The Mysteries of Pittsburgh*, and [in *Wonder Boys*] the strange subterranean woman who puts records on in the bar the writers frequent late at night, but more specifically that tuba case! These objects become simultaneously significant and trivial. They're the understructure of the narrative but they're also jokes.

Chabon: Yes, you're right. Certain things tend to appear in the narrative, and once they're there, they keep reappearing, almost in a way that I'm not really that deliberate about, but each time they reappear maybe I put another little spin on the description of it or the way that the characters talk about it or think about it. I don't intend them to be at all symbolic but they do accrue a kind of meaning as they travel through the book or as the characters rotate around them.

Silverblatt: Let me give an example. At the beginning of *Wonder Boys*, the narrator Grady Tripp is meeting his editor, the somewhat diabolic Crabtree, at the airport. Crabtree has met what we are led to believe is probably a transvestite on board the airplane. She has mysteriously transvestite luggage as well. She's dressed her bags up as much as she has altered herself imaginatively. Among her questionable effects is a tuba case which we're never sure is hers and which turns out in fact to be empty. This figure, this arrival of

what feels like the devil, Crabtree, or at least some kind of devil figure, with this strange man-woman with an empty tuba case, reminded me something in *The Master and Margarita*. But of course as I read I was absolutely expecting, being a devotee of farce, for the mysterious transvestite, who's gone for most of the novel, to reappear. In a farce, she would, and would take her place in the inevitable mechanism. What allowed you not to resuscitate her?
Chabon: Maybe it was that tuba. [*laughter*] If we have her tuba then we don't need her, and the tuba keeps bobbing back up to the surface over and over again. I thought about it—I asked myself if she would make another appearance in the book, and I decided no, she wouldn't.

Silverblatt: This would be too clean.
Chabon: Yeah. As the book goes on, Grady is driving around Pittsburgh in this huge old Ford Galaxie convertible and his trunk begins to fill up very quickly with lots of different kinds of objects, most of which are the product of another terrible mistake that he's made, and once I had his trunk filled up then I realized I had to get him through the process of emptying of again and disposing of each of those objects. I had to do all of that and I had to bring Grady safely home again and take care of all the other characters, and I did think it was going to make it the story seem too much of a mechanical contrivance to tie up Miss Sloviak as well.

Silverblatt: Now, the objects that accumulate in his trunk are the product of yet another mistake that he's made, as you say. In his life he seems to have accumulated mistakes as well: three wives and a whole lot of imperviousness that allows him, for instance, to see a young writing student of his holding a revolver—that turns out not to be a toy—to his head in the backyard and to let that young man go without medical attention, as well as to let a wounded ankle that he's gotten himself to go without medical attention. Everything is being left in some unexamined trunk in this book, and those objects seem to function as the things he doesn't look at but simply accrues. It's a comedy of the serious guilt of his life.
Chabon: Yeah, that's good. What he has to do in this book is finally unload that trunk and take responsibility for the things that he's done. In the case of that ankle of his he has to finally attend to that, and he's also been ignoring the fact that he's having these bizarre dizzy spells for the past several weeks before the book begins. He has a number of them during the book, and that's another thing that he finally has to face. To me, I think the book is much less about writer's block, because Grady's problem is sort of the

opposite of writer's block. He'd probably be better off if he had a little bout of writer's block—it would probably be good for him. He can't seem to stop producing material. But what I think it's about is this very thing, facing the trunk full of stuff that he is carrying around behind him and facing the nature of who he is at this point in his life, having been in a way a wonder boy at some point and carrying around all that baggage with him, and now arriving at a point when he's forty-four years old and he isn't that any more, but he has never faced that either. I think that is one explanation for why his life is such a mess—he is still trying to live like a twenty-two-year-old when he is a forty-four-year-old with three marriages and a job as a professor and things that he needs to take seriously that he doesn't.

Silverblatt: From the tone of your work I would think that you'd say that growing up is the hardest imaginable thing to do. Can you speak about that?
Chabon: I don't know. Maybe if I were speaking personally I would say that I feel as though I've grown up without ever having really tried to, exactly. And that was maybe because my parents were divorced when I was about eleven or twelve, and I lived with my mom and I kind of had to start taking a share of the responsibilities of the house, and I started to grow up at least in some ways fairly early. And yet, at the same time, I feel as though, looking around at men my age, friends of mine with whom I have so much in common, I see that in a lot of ways they are in that position of not wanting to grow up, so then it makes me maybe wonder about myself. I don't know if it's the hardest thing to do or if it's kind of the last thing that our culture demands of a man.

Silverblatt: The last frontier. There's also a kind of character who reappears who I find very appealing, the charming liar or deceiver. He's there in Arthur in *Mysteries*, he's here in Crabtree, where it's not so much lying as the invention of sudden solutions—it's his gift. And it's what makes me think, as I say, of the appearance of the devil. In most fiction the devil is the figure who has that kind of complicated delicious syntax, who can bring anything into a sentence and is constantly working magic tricks. Could you speak about that figure?
Chabon: Well, I think also you're forgetting James Leer in this book, who is an even worse liar or a better liar than Crabtree. I see that in my stories too. There's a story about a colossal instance of plagiarism, a massive deception. I'm interested in liars. I always have been. The play *Six Degrees of Separation* is a great play, and it's because of that character. I've always been interested in people who say they're one thing and turn out to be another thing. I don't

know why—it's just a motif that interests me, and then they are fun to write. It's very entertaining to write a character who you get to actually give two biographies to, or two realities, or more—who's not limited by the actual facts of their birth and upbringing, but you can invent for them, under the guise of their inventing it for themselves, any kind of fantastic destiny.

Silverblatt: It's also very American for some reason. I think I first encountered and fell in love with that kind of character in the movie musical *The Music Man*, the person who speaks in complicated patter-like sentences—
Chabon: Professor Harold Hill.

Silverblatt: —Harold Hill, hoodwinking everyone. But of course we have Melville's *The Confidence-Man*—
Chabon: *The Great Gatsby*.

Silverblatt: It seems as if it's an American theme, an American theme about growing up. *Huckleberry Finn* is full of those disguises.
Chabon: The Duke and the Dauphin.

Silverblatt: But Huck himself dresses as a girl and says that his mother is dying. So I wondered why con artists are so appealing?
Chabon: Well, it has a lot to do with narrative, I think. A con is a story, and I like to try to find ways to tell as many stories as possible, or to find as many different possible outlets within one novel, say, for the narrative impulse to come out. Plot to me is the maybe the least interesting part of the job, although I try my best to come up with serviceable ones for my books. That way of creating a narrative interests me a lot less than somehow finding other ways of doing it, and I think a con artist—the trickster character, the Loki character—is a way to sort of create another kind of narrative that can exist within your larger one that is a lot more entertaining for me as a writer.

Silverblatt: Yes, and in a sense of course, a transvestite is a con person of another sort, and in a way the empty tuba case is like those empty shells that street mountebanks manipulate—when will the cover be lifted and finally you will find something full? It's sort of funny in this book because there's a full trunk but with an empty box inside, and there is that sense of a person as being someone who is simultaneously full and empty, self-invented and avoiding everything at the same time.
Chabon: Yeah, emptiness and then fullness is definitely a motif in the book.

It's not something I planned, but going back over it, I notice there are empty houses and empty suitcases and empty graves and empty beds. There's a line about the next empty bedroom. Emptiness seems to be a theme. And then I notice that Grady has a conscious thought about emptiness, and he ties it in with the writer that was the first formative influence on him as a writer in his life, which was the upstairs neighbor in the house he grew up in, a writer named Albert Vetch who wrote under the name August Van Zorn, who wrote horror stories in which over and over again some unsuspecting young foolish professor or researcher would come face to face with this horrible emptiness that bites your head off. So, emptiness is there in the book.

Silverblatt: And there in life as well.
Chabon: Yes indeed.

Silverblatt: It does seem that at the end of this quest what Grady Tripp discovers is the emptiness of his life, or what has become an emptied-out life.
Chabon: He's known it for quite a while but he finally faces it.

Interview with Michael Chabon

Bob Goodman / 1996

From *Beacon Street Review* 9.2 (1996): 39–45. Reprinted by permission.

Michael Chabon burst onto the literary scene at the age of twenty-four with the 1988 bestseller *The Mysteries of Pittsburgh*, an accomplished debut about a sexually confused summer in the life of recent college graduate Art Bechstein. Last year, Chabon delivered a long-awaited and worthy follow-up, *Wonder Boys*, in which Grady Tripp, a pot-addled writer and college teacher, sees his marriage, his teaching post, his 2,600-page novel, and his claim to the Wonder Boy mantle come unglued in the course of a single weekend. Both books defied the proclaimed death of American letters, showing that commercial success and literary merit are not always mutually exclusive.

In the seven intervening years, Chabon (pronounced "SHAY-bahn") published the critically acclaimed though commercially unsuccessful *A Model World*, a 1991 collection of short stories, many of which had been published in the *New Yorker*. And he worked on another novel called *Fountain City* before deciding to abandon it altogether after 700 pages. "I had certain key elements that I couldn't get to mesh, no matter how hard I tried," he said in a recent interview. His lyrical writing style is filled with dense descriptive passages and labyrinthine sentences that yield rich rewards to intrepid readers. His style and angst-ridden suburban subject matter have earned him comparisons to both F. Scott Fitzgerald and John Updike. But the comparisons leave out a key ingredient of Chabon's recipe: his out-of-the-closet sexual ambiguity. Male bonding in his work is fraught with knowing sexual chemistry, though his characters defy easy categories of sexual orientation. "All male friendships," says *Wonder Boys'* first-person narrator, "are essentially quixotic: they last only so long as each man is willing to polish the donkey helmet, climb on his donkey, and ride off after each other in pursuit of elusive glory and questionable adventure."

Chabon grew up in Columbia, Maryland, the elder of two brothers. His mother, Sharon, now a lawyer, and father, Robert, a doctor, lawyer, and direc-

16

tor of a medical center, divorced when he was eleven, a traumatic event he has described as "the worst thing that ever happened to me." He went to the University of Pittsburgh as an undergraduate and received his master's degree in creative writing from the University of California at Irvine.

Today Chabon, thirty-two, lives in Los Angeles with his wife, Ayelet Waldman, a lawyer and teacher, and their baby daughter, Sophie. He recently completed two screenplays, one a romantic comedy optioned by Paramount and the other a science fiction feature sold to Fox, and he's now back at work on fiction. We spoke in February when he was in Boston to promote the paperback release of *Wonder Boys*. The soft-spoken and unassuming author touched on many subjects, including his fascination with male friendships, the roots of his writing style, and the growing role of Jewish material in his work.

BG: Are you working on a new novel?

Chabon: Yes, I just started in December and I've got about 100 pages. It's set in New York during the so-called Golden Age of the comic book. It starts in 1938 with the appearance of Superman and ends sometime around the early fifties with the Comics Code imposition and the collapse of the comic book business for several years. I collected comic books when I was a kid.

BG: When did you write your first story?

Chabon: When I was thirteen, I wrote a story for a class assignment. I wrote a pastiche of Arthur Conan Doyle with Sherlock Holmes meeting Captain Nemo from *Twenty Thousand Leagues Under the Sea*. It was fun. I loved it. I really tried to write like Doyle and copy his style. I got a lot of good response from my parents and my teacher and so on. From that point on, I considered myself a writer in the making, though I didn't write with any kind of regularity or discipline. It was a fitful kind of thing.

BG: In your short story collection, *A Model World*, the young Nathan Shapiro character and the breakup of his family seem to be culled from your own childhood. Were you nervous about reactions from family members?

Chabon: Well, a little bit. For the most part, I had never communicated to my parents my feelings about their divorce. It had always been the accepted wisdom in our family that it was for the best. And I think it was for the best, generally speaking. Certainly, from the point of view of my parents, they were much happier. But there was obviously a lot of pain associated with it for me, and my brother, too. I think we had kept it to ourselves. So they were surprised to find the degree to which it had hurt. I think it had been clear to them at first and then they assumed I got over it, and I did, obviously, but still, I carry it around with me to this day.

BG: The theme of quixotic male friendships runs throughout your work. What is it about the subject that holds so much allure for you?

Chabon: I don't think I really know the answer to that question. In a sense, I prefer not to think about it too much because obviously it's a valuable source of material for me and I'm afraid if I look into it too much it might lose some of its mystery. I seem to choose to tell stories—and it feels like the stories choose me—about men and their relations and their friendships. While there certainly is a rich literature of this going back to the *Iliad*, where it's men as equals or relations between fathers and sons—which goes back to the Greeks, too—I feel it's always been handled in a certain way. It's been a very "male" way, with a limited range of feeling and vocabulary, although still rich. But I feel there's plenty of room for new approaches to the material. It seems the relationship between men and women has been covered from every conceivable style and point of view. The relationship between men hasn't been thoroughly explored by writers who have the freedom to consider the full spectrum, from father and son to two male lovers, and view it as a continuum.

BG: What's different about your male characters is that they are aware of a sexual attraction, while historically in literature that's been in the lurking subtext as something that generally the author is unaware of or refuses to acknowledge.

Chabon: Right. Exactly. Exactly. And I feel that, having been granted the freedom by society to explore this, I have to try and take advantage of it.

BG: Your writing style bucks the trend toward minimalism and Hemingway-style prose. How did your style evolve?

Chabon: It didn't happen spontaneously. I've always liked reading writers who have an involved, metaphorical, grammatically complicated style with a rich vocabulary. Those have been my favorites, writers like Nabokov, John Cheever, and Jorge Luis Borges, Updike and Marcel Proust. Another writer I really love is S. J. Perelman, who had a brilliant vocabulary and was a genius with metaphor and simile, although what he tended to do was try to explode his metaphors and similes. So I responded to, and early on imitated, those writers. At this point, it's not at all a conscious or imitative thing. I'll start writing a sentence with a general idea I want to say "x" about this character, and before I know it, it's 135 words long, and I've broken it up with a few parentheticals and something between dashes, and it just happens that way.

BG: Your writing is spiced with pop-culture references. You seem to have an almost encyclopedic knowledge. Where does that come from?

Chabon: Encyclopedism is definitely part of my family. First and foremost, there's my father, who knows everything and has an immense variety of facts at his fingertips, and at times in his life has deliberately set out to master various branches of knowledge and learned what he could about them. That was always extremely valuable to me, too. I read the encyclopedia when I was a kid for fun. And I read the dictionary for fun. I discovered that I had fortunately inherited from my father his memory for things like that, so very quickly my brain began to fill up with all this stuff. I just can't help it, in a sense.

There is a tradition in literature, the encyclopedist impulse, to pack as much as you possibly can into a book, with writers as diverse as Cervantes, Rabelais, and then coming down to Thomas Pynchon and Nabokov, both of whose books are laced with references. I respond as a reader to that, and therefore my ideal reader responds, too, and that's who I'm writing for, someone a lot like me. I love getting the response from readers who spot the reference and write to tell me so.

BG: There's a hilarious scene in *Wonder Boys* revolving around a Passover Seder and Grady's wry observations. So here you are, a Jewish man playing a Gentile man observing Jewish culture. Did that stance give you more freedom to explore Jewish issues?

Chabon: It definitely did. It was fun, but also crucial, to my being able to deal with this material that I approach it from the point of view of a gentile. Because the communal angst of that Seder dinner table is my angst. And I couldn't have written about it as a participant in it. There are all those ancient feelings of bewilderment, resentment, and anger that are perhaps embodied best by that rabble of Israelites wandering through the desert, following after Moses because he tells them to, and constantly backsliding and worshiping idols every chance they get. The symbols of the Seder plate are so well known to me and so deeply a part of who I am that I had to be Grady to be able to look at it and say, "That is the most bizarre assortment of stuff on a plate. What kind of a meal is that? It's ridiculous." I could have done it myself, but being Grady helped immeasurably.

BG: In terms of being a Jewish writer, your style and influences are very different from the standard-bearers like Roth, Malamud, and Bellow. Do they interest you as writers?

Chabon: Oh, definitely. They saw themselves as American writers and very aggressively, as the children of immigrants, wanted to insert themselves into American literature. I think the difference is for them, they had to prove they were Americans. And I don't have to prove that. I can't help it. I'm completely

American, through and through, and I embrace it. Now the situation is sort of reversed and I have to prove I'm a Jew. I remember—it's stuck in my mind like a burr for years now—that once someone wrote an article in a Jewish paper in northern California about young Jewish writers. They call Cynthia Ozick [Jewish short story writer and essayist] for comment and she said, about me, specifically: He may be Jewish and he may be a writer, but he's not a Jewish writer. That just stung me, because I thought it was a stupid thing to say from a very intelligent woman whose writing I admire greatly, and because it rang true. I knew what she meant. I realized that before I could have someone like Cynthia Ozick judge me differently, I would have to establish to myself to what degree I was a Jewish writer. I had just taken it for granted, and I was forced to think about it. I'll probably go on wrestling with it for some time. I've joined the eternal debate over who is a Jew.

BG: In the *Washington Post*, Jonathan Yardley wrote a glowing review of *Wonder Boys*, but he also urged you to dig deeper, saying in part: "Though Chabon has demonstrated a keen understanding of other people's minds and lives, thus far his preoccupation has been with fictional explorations of his own. It is time for him to move, to break away from first person and explore larger worlds." How do you respond?

Chabon: I don't believe the specific point was correct. I think there's a huge difference between the first-person narration of *Mysteries* and that of *Wonder Boys*. In the case of *Mysteries*, it is, as he says, the kind of expected semi-confessional first novel, a narrator close in many ways to myself. In *Wonder Boys*, though, it's much more an act of impersonation. The only similarity between me and Grady is that we both got lost in books. Other than that, we're totally different. So I don't feel like I did two early stepping-stone narrations.

But I see his point in that I don't think either book is especially broad in scope or ambitious in terms of structure, story, and narrative. They both take place over a limited period of time, one over a summer and the other over a weekend. One of the things I would like to do is become more ambitious and carry out that ambition, to work toward the great novelistic ideal represented by *Middlemarch* or *War and Peace*. I'll never be able to do anything like them, but that model is something to move toward, which demands a third-person narration. I choose to interpret his exhortation to move toward the third person as also extending to all the things third person makes possible.

BG: In the book you're working on now, are you in first or third person?

Chabon: Third, by chance. [*Laughs.*] It just so happens.

Interview: Michael Chabon

Scott Tobias / 2000

From *The Onion A.V. Club*, 22 November 2000. www.avclub.com. Reprinted by permission.

In his mid-twenties, as a creative writing graduate student at the University of California at Irvine, Michael Chabon submitted as his master's thesis a brisk novel about a confused young man coming to terms with his sexuality. Needless to say, he earned the degree, but his professor was so impressed with Chabon's work that he immediately sent it along to his agent. The book, 1988's *The Mysteries of Pittsburgh*, earned rave reviews on its way to becoming a bestseller. Chabon spent much of the early '90s working on a highly ambitious opus called *Fountain City*, about an architect building a perfect baseball park in Florida, but he scrapped the project after failing to give shape to the thousands of pages he had written. From the ashes of that experience rose 1995's *Wonder Boys*, an evocative comic novel that channeled his frustrations into the main character, a professor and author whose own much-anticipated sophomore effort is running well into the thousands, with no end in sight. This year's pitch-perfect film adaptation of *Wonder Boys*, directed by Curtis Hanson (*L.A. Confidential*) and starring Michael Douglas, failed to make much of an impression at the box office, but enthusiastic notices prompted a re-release in some cities. Chabon's latest and most ambitious novel, *The Amazing Adventures of Kavalier & Clay*, chronicles the rise of two Jewish cousins who write comic books during the "Golden Age" in the late '30s and '40s. Sammy Klayman, an opportunistic young man with a knack for pulp plotting, is perfectly complemented by Czech émigré Josef Kavalier, whose bold drawing style lends new sophistication and power to the medium. Together, with the help of costumed creations such as the Harry Houdini–inspired The Escapist, they fight the war on the page. Chabon recently spoke to *The Onion A.V. Club* about his early devotion to comic books, his proposal for an *X-Men* movie script, and the unexpected perils of writing fiction.

The Onion: What is your history as a reader of comic books?

Michael Chabon: I was introduced to them pretty early, right around the age of six or so, by my father, who had himself been a devoted reader of comics when he was a child. His father was a typographer in New York, and he worked at a plant where they printed comic books, so he used to come home with bags full of them for my father to read as a kid growing up in Brooklyn. So I guess when I started reading, my father thought it was only natural that I should take an interest in comic books, too, and he started bringing me comics to read, although he wasn't getting them for free. I read mostly DC Comics at that time, which was the late '60s and early '70s. They were still very much what they had been for many years: somewhat naïve, innocent, primary-colored, and set in a world with very clear distinctions between good and evil. And that was very appealing to me when I was little. As I got older, I switched over to the Marvel world, where things were murkier and more ambiguous and the heroes had the famous "feet of clay" and more human foibles and failings. And I think that's more appealing to an older kid. Then, when I was a teenager, I completely lost interest in comics, sold my collection, forgot all about them for fifteen years or so, and had to reeducate myself again to write [*Kavalier & Clay*].

Onion: What was your first introduction to the so-called "Golden Age" of the medium?

Chabon: Actually, it came in my reading of DC Comics in the late '60s and early '70s, because at that time, DC published several different lines of so-called "giant" comics that were somewhere between fifty-two and one hundred pages. And to fill out those big comic books, they reprinted all kinds of material, and a lot of it was Golden Age stuff. So I got exposed to it directly through the pages of a comic book—not through an old compilation book at the library or something, but actually pulpy, stapled comics with the adventures of heroes from the late '30s, '40s, and into the early '50s. A lot of it was exactly the same stuff my dad had read as a kid, so we were able to talk about them, and that formed a very important early connection of taste between us.

Onion: When your interest in reading comics waned, was that a consequence of adulthood or the failure of comics to make that transition with you?

Chabon: I think I outgrew them the way a lot of other people do. I just got interested in reading other things around the time I was fourteen or fifteen. I also stopped reading science fiction and fantasy and started on so-called adult fiction, stuff my parents would recommend to me that they were enjoying. My tastes changed, and I was more interested in reading literature and contemporary fiction than I was in genre fiction and comic books.

Onion: Well, the reason I ask is that it's such a concern in the book, this idea of comics as a medium for adults, and the problems it has making that transition.

Chabon: At the time I was giving up on comics in the mid- to late '70s, there wasn't much in the way of what are now called "graphic novels" or adult comics. There was the underground stuff, like *Zap Comix* with Robert Crumb and *Fabulous Furry Freak Brothers*, but that didn't really appeal to me. Had there been artists around like Daniel Clowes or Chris Ware, I don't know if I'd have kept reading or not. It's hard to say.

Onion: Why do you feel such an affection for Jack Kirby [creator or co-creator of the Incredible Hulk, Captain America, Iron Man, Spider-Man, and Fantastic Four]?

Chabon: He was really the first comic book artist I learned to identify by sight. His work was very distinctive, so it was not like a great feat of discernment on my part. But as a kid of six or seven, I was thrilled by his unique stylization, and he was the first one I learned to spot without having seen who had drawn the particular comic I was reading. So that was the first initial impulse. He had this astonishingly fertile imagination where he generated and shed concepts and ideas and nomenclatures . . . In the course of a single comic book, he would create and destroy an entire universe that he had richly peopled with races and worlds. Then, in the very next issue, he'd do it all over again. I think that kind of inexhaustible fertility really appealed to me. Even to this day, I continue to revere him along with other heroes of mine, like Nikola Tesla, the great inventor, whom I also see as somehow having tapped into this amazing, mysterious supply of imagination.

Onion: What were the particular historical models you had in mind for *Kavalier & Clay*?

Chabon: I didn't really have any specific models. Neither of the main characters is based in particular on any one or even any couple of actual comic book creators. It was more, especially in Sammy's case, that there was an easy pattern to be discerned among creators at the time. Many of them, not all, were young Jewish guys from New York with immigrant parents, a yen for success, and a love of the pulps. All of those qualities were pretty common among comic book men at the time, almost universal, and so it was not basing Sammy on any one person, but on the archetype of the comic book creator. In the case of Joe, I don't see him as being based on anybody, or even fitting a particular pattern. The only thing I would say about him that I really did draw from an actual creator is that I gave him Will Eisner's rather surprising and unshakable faith in the medium of comic books. That was rare at the time. In fact, I think Eisner was unique in feeling from the start that comic books were not necessarily this despised, bastard, crappy, low-brow kind of art form, and that there was a potential for real art. And he saw that from the very beginning, which was very unusual, and I took that quality and gave it to Joe Kavalier. I think that was the only direct borrowing I really did.

Onion: What did you find was comic books' predominant attitude toward the war?

Chabon: Well, they were incredibly jingoistic, just rife with horrifically gross caricatures of Japanese and Germans. The entire comic book world went to war, and it went to war a little earlier than the United States actually did, for the most part. Throughout the war, that was pretty much the single theme of almost every superhero comic book: the war, saboteurs, fighting the Axis Powers. Without the war, I don't know if comic books would have caught on the way they did. They were the perfect medium for the time, and the boys and girls of America really responded to this sort of fantasy fighting. I think those children were keenly aware of the actual war being fought, because family members of theirs were fighting in it or were somehow or other victimized by it. I think it was very appealing to kids at the time, who were so painfully conscious of the war, to have this fantasy war going on, which could be easily won over and over again by these costumed heroes.

Onion: When you talked to various comic book artists while researching the book, did you find them as conflicted as Kavalier is in their relationship to violence?

Chabon: I didn't really ask them about it that much. When I was interviewing those guys, I was in the fairly early stages of writing the book, and at that point, I was more concerned with getting their help in painting a portrait of the time and the features of their lives at the time. So I was asking them things like what they wore, and where they worked, and what their offices were like, and how they got there: Did they ride the bus or take the street-cars? Those kinds of things, and also how they started working, how they worked, what kind of brushes they used, and all of those more quotidian things. So a thematic concern like [their relationship to the violence in their work] hadn't occurred to me yet. I wasn't immersed in the material enough. The question of violence and the inherent fascistic nature of the superhero didn't really come to me so early. I had to grow into it and look at it through the point of view of Joe Kavalier. It was only once I was immersed in his character that it started to be a concern of mine. That said, I did find it to be a concern in interviews I later read with creators, especially someone like Eisner, who is one of the more thoughtful people ever to work in comics. He didn't address the issue as overtly as Joe does in the novel, but he did touch on the fact that he had dressed his famous team of aviators, the Blackhawks, in uniforms that were consciously modeled on SS stormtrooper uniforms. He said he was somehow responding to some element in the look of the Nazi forces that seemed right for these so-called heroic characters, too. So that gave me sort of a confirmation about what I was having Joe think and feel about what he was doing. But it's certainly not an original idea of mine. If you look at a work like Alan Moore's *Watchmen*, the whole idea of the superhero as fascist gets a real working-over.

Onion: After your experience with *Fountain City*, were you nervous about leaping into a project of this proportion?

Chabon: Yeah, I was a little bit, and there were definitely times while I was working on it when I worried I had done it again. I did run into some rough patches, and in the course of trying to get through them, I couldn't help but wonder if I had done it to myself all over again. But it was never really the same, because I felt from the first that there was just something about this time, this place, and the business of comic books that was so real and juicy. It wasn't like *Fountain City*, where I never felt like I was conceptually on steady ground, and I was trying to knit together these disparate elements in the hope it would add up to something. With [*Kavalier & Clay*], I felt from the very beginning that there was this fundamental kernel from which you could make a novel.

Onion: Did your writing habits change? Were there other lessons you took from the experience?

Chabon: No, I've always had pretty good habits. I don't think I could have worked on *Fountain City* for five years and generated as much material as I did if I didn't have steady work habits. I think that if I learned anything, it's that you can feel completely despairing and hopeless and in over your head and lost and incompetent in the course of writing a book, but that doesn't mean all those things are true. You can fight your way through those periods to a new appreciation of what you're doing and to a firmer grip on the material. If I had known that with *Fountain City*, I might have fought just a little longer to try to pull it together.

Onion: Will elements of that book—I'm thinking of the baseball angle, in particular—find their way into future works?

Chabon: I don't know. As you mention, the baseball angle was the initial exciting idea for me, and it had been completely superseded by reality. When I first came up with *Fountain City*, the idea of a downtown, green-grass, baseball-only, intimate sort of Ebbets Field/Fenway Park-style stadium being built in a contemporary setting was a complete fantasy, and it seemed like such a wonderful idea to me. But in the course of writing that book, I first started hearing of this new park they were building in Baltimore. Then they built it and started working on another one in Cleveland, and so on. So reality completely caught up to me. Now, [building old-style baseball parks] is old hat, which takes away one of the central pillars of that book.

Onion: Were you concerned about the tone of *Kavalier & Clay*? On the one hand, it's a brisk and adventurous yarn, while on the other, it does deal with a lot of the darker issues related to the war.

Chabon: No. Tone is definitely not something I worry about too much. I feel that in the past, my style has shown itself to be capable of handling dark and light in the same paragraph, or even in the same sentence. That's something I almost take for granted now. I think it was more a concern to get the details right and persuasively re-create the world I was trying to write about.

Onion: What is your history in creative writing classes? It seems like so many books I've read lately have the same attitude about them, which is that those who have it have it, and that no amount of guidance or instruction will make a difference to those who don't. Do you find that to be the case?

Chabon: It depends on what you mean by "it," I suppose. [*Laughs.*] I don't know if you've looked at this new book by Stephen King, *On Writing*, but he talks about how instruction of this kind couldn't make a bad writer into a good writer and it couldn't make a good writer into a great writer, but it can take someone who has a certain amount of innate ability and help them avoid lots of common pitfalls. I don't think you could teach someone to be a genius, but you can certainly teach them to not make rookie mistakes and to look at writing the way a writer looks at writing, and not just the way a reader looks at writing. There are a lot of techniques and skills that can be taught that will be helpful to anybody, no matter how gifted they are, and I think writing programs can be very good for people. It always seemed strange to me that this question gets raised only in the context of the teaching of writing, as though writing were different from the other arts, which have routinely been taught for a long time, like music and painting and drama and sculpting.

Onion: It seems like all these disciplines have been questioned because they don't have, for lack of a better term, practical applications. In math, there's always a single answer to a problem that can be taught. With the arts, you're dealing more with vagaries.

Chabon: Yeah, but they should still be taught. Painting, for example, is full of techniques that you would only learn if somebody showed you how to do them. And that's true for writing, too. Let's just take the question of point of view in fiction, with first-person, third-person, limited point of view, omniscient point of view, and so forth. Somebody who's out there, reading on his or her own and trying to become a writer, may conceivably read for years and never really get quickly to the bottom of the issue of point of view in fiction, and the difficulties and advantages to adopting one point of view over another. Now, a truly gifted writer might have an intuitive grasp of that and not need to have it demonstrated through careful reading of selected works that illustrate point of view very well. But I think it's really helpful for a lot of writers, and from what little teaching I've done, it can be eye-opening to just take a piece of fiction and look at it exclusively for point of view. You can take a work like, say, *Lolita* and not look at it for what it's about, or what's happening, or how beautiful the language is, or the scenes of innocence and experience and corruption. If you just examine the question of point of view, which is not naturally something a reader would do on his or her own, it can be incredibly instructive and informative. It can really help you in your own work when it comes time for you to attempt, for example, some kind of a strange, unreliable first-person narrator.

Onion: To what do you attribute the indifferent popular response to the film version of *Wonder Boys*?

Chabon: Of course, I kind of blame myself. One can't help but think that all these talented people, from the screenwriter to the director to the cast to the producer to the cinematographer, put all their amazing gifts and hard work into something that was fundamentally not worthy of them. But I also think that it was kind of a tricky pitch. It was hard to figure out how to market that film and find what kind of audience it would appeal to. And I guess they didn't really solve those admittedly very difficult problems. Also, it came out in February, which is sort of a dead time of year.

Onion: Watching a film like that fail to make money, you have to wonder how studios can sell films for adults in a climate that's really teen-oriented.

Chabon: I think [*Wonder Boys*] is a film for adults, but on the other hand, that's almost like the kiss of death in a way. It's weird. Supposedly, there are adults out there who are hungry for films that aren't aimed at teens, but where are they? Why don't they go see a movie like that when every reviewer in the country—for the most part, anyway—is telling them that this is a movie for you and not for the *Scream/I Know What You Did Last Summer* crowd? But they didn't turn out for it, which makes you wonder whether the whole idea of a film for adults is a canard or something. The campaign was aimed at more grown-up people. The trailer had a more sophisticated touch to it: You had to read along with it as you were watching. And they had that great Bob Dylan song, which you'd think would appeal, for lack of a better term, to the VH1 generation. And yet, with all of that, it still didn't get across somehow. Whether that was the fault of the studio or the fault of the adults who supposedly want to go see movies about themselves, I don't know. It's almost as if a film like that needs cachet, and yet the adult crowd to whom a film like that might appeal is somehow incapable of bestowing cachet. Cachet definitely seems like something that arises exclusively from the younger crowd.

Onion: Reading your proposal for the *X-Men* script, it sounds like a lot of your general ideas about what it should be—to reveal the X-Men universe through Wolverine's eyes, dispensing with supervillains, and so on—made it into the film.

Chabon: But they didn't dispense with the idea of supervillains. I think they flew directly in the face of what I was suggesting. They had Magneto and Toad and Mystique. . . . It was loaded with supervillains. I was saying, "No

Magneto." Magneto had been there in every previous draft that I read, and they're all kind of collectively known as "The Brotherhood of Evil Mutants." I thought that was a big mistake. It was hard enough to keep track of all the heroes among the X-Men. And as far as doing it from Wolverine's point of view, that didn't originate with me. That was sort of a given. I took it as a given, because it was more or less an element in most of the prior drafts I'd read. It just seemed like a natural, I suppose, because he's not a team player and they are a team. So it seemed like an inevitable way of setting up the story, to have this outside, lone-wolf type who encounters this functioning unit and is ultimately accepted by them and accepts them.

Onion: Why do you imagine your proposal was rejected?
Chabon: Oh, it was a very simple reason. When [director] Bryan Singer and his screenwriting partner, Christopher McQuarrie, came along, the studio very wisely dropped me like a hot potato.

Onion: There were no particular objections to your ideas?
Chabon: No. In fact, I think I was on the verge of getting hired. I was trying to reassure a couple of people who had a few reservations, and as I was engaged in that process, Bryan Singer showed up. And he was hot off *The Usual Suspects,* as was Christopher McQuarrie. So getting rid of me was a no-brainer, as they say.

Onion: How have your struggles to break into television been working out?
Chabon: I wrote a pilot [*House of Gold*] for CBS, which was not picked up, unfortunately. And now, I'm just starting to work on the second one for TNT. At this point, I'm batting .000. But who knows? Maybe by next year, I'll be batting .500.

Onion: Putting aside the obvious problems of creating a show for a network, the medium itself seems to hold a lot of potential, particularly for a novelist.
Chabon: I agree. There's something inherently more appealing about the idea that you could reveal and tell stories about characters over the course of a TV season—thirteen or twenty-six episodes, whatever it might be—than in the course of one two-hour movie. You can do so many more novelistic kinds of things on a TV show—with time, with gradual development of relationships, and so on—than you could possibly do in a movie. And that is very appealing.

Onion: And *House of Gold* has an original and intriguing premise, covering three different generations in one family over three different time periods.
Chabon: Yeah, I thought it was a cool idea, too. If you ever find yourself to be a programming executive at a major network, let me know. [*Laughs.*]

Onion: For an idea so novel, didn't you want to shop it around at more ambitious outlets, like HBO?
Chabon: There was some talk about it, but it didn't really seem like the producers I was working with quite had the energy for that. Or maybe I didn't, either. We thought about going to HBO or Showtime, but it didn't seem like it had the quote-unquote—and I'm putting quotes on there very deliberately—"edge" that those kinds of networks favor in what they do run.

Onion: Yeah, but it doesn't seem like the kind of thing that would come out of the network that brought you *Big Brother* or *Bette.*
Chabon: No. They said—or somebody said they said—that they wanted more adventuresome shows that would help them capture an audience they hadn't been able to capture at that point. They were still the *Touched by an Angel* and *Murder, She Wrote* network. But ultimately, it didn't turn out that way, at least as far as I was concerned.

Onion: What are some of the problems of being a novelist in this particular time? What gratification do you get from the release of a book, especially in a time when it's destined to be dwarfed in sales by the likes of a Ludlum or Clancy?
Chabon: I guess I don't really look at it that way. The problems you have as a novelist tend to have to do with making a living and trying to find ways to supplement the income you get from writing novels. For a lot of writers, that involves teaching. In my case, so far, I've been able to get by working in Hollywood with this TV stuff I've been doing. And it's very important, because my wife is a writer, too, and we don't have health insurance through any employer. Therefore, our health insurance comes through the screenwriter's guild, so I can only ensure my family's health by working in Hollywood. In a way, that's a problem for me, because I'd much prefer to be writing novels all the time. But from the point of view of the marketplace for novels, I want my book to do well, and I want my publisher to be happy with me and to feel like I'm a good bet. But for me, the goal is always to write a novel that I myself would like to read. People frequently ask me what my favorite book is, and in effect, there's always a capital-F Favorite, capital-B Book that I would like

to write myself someday. I try to go for that ideal of writing the best, most entertaining, most beautifully written book that I possibly can. So I never get too upset. I just go into it expecting that I'm never going to be a Tom Clancy. And I wouldn't really want to be—not that I have anything against him, and I wish him continued success—because that's not why I'm writing novels. I'm doing it because I have to. I feel like I have to, anyway.

Michael Chabon

Michael Silverblatt / 2000

From *Bookworm*. KCRW, Santa Monica, CA, 7 December 2000. © KCRW *Bookworm*. Web. http://www.kcrw.com/etc/programs/bw. Reprinted by permission. Michael Silverblatt is coproducer and host of KCRW's *Bookworm*.

Michael Silverblatt: Welcome to *Bookworm*. Today my guest is Michael Chabon. He is the author of *The Amazing Adventures of Kavalier & Clay*, published by Random House. It is his third novel, and its events, which center around the Golden Age of Comic Books, include many visiting heroes, including Houdini and Salvador Dali, but in particular the invented creators of a comic book called *The Escapist*. Michael, where do comic books begin for you? Where did your involvement with them start?

Michael Chabon: When I was six or seven, my father started to bring me comic books to read. They had been a very important part of his childhood. My grandfather—his father—was a printer who worked in a plant on the west side of New York where they printed comic books. He worked the night shift, and he would regularly come home in the morning with big bags full of comic books that he had somehow obtained at work, and my dad would consume them in a single night and then trade them in at the candy store on the corner in Brooklyn for other titles. He became a really voracious reader of comics. So I think he was just waiting for me to finally be old enough to read them so he would have an excuse to start buying them again himself. And in fact he did—he would read them before he gave them to me, and then I would read them, and then we would talk about them. It became an early form of discourse between us, something that we could share, and it led me to a greater interest in the period that I'm writing about in this book. My father is of an age to have been a reader of the comics of Kavalier and Clay. And his interest in the popular culture of his own childhood and of the time before was very successfully transmitted to me, so that it was always a

32

period that I've wanted to write about. I was really just looking for an excuse to finally find a subject.

Silverblatt: The first time I became aware of the Jewish undertext of comic books was an essay by Leslie Fiedler, who talked about how it was two Jewish boys who had invented Superman, and they were geeks, and that Superman represented a kind of projection of the dual nature of the geek and the WASP. And this book, too, emphasizes some of the Jewish origins of comics, ranging from Houdini, which is the first time I've ever connected Houdini with comics—I think it's quite a wonderful perception, the escape artist—and the figure of the golem that appears in the first chapter. What do you think it is that makes this a kind of Jewish . . . ?
Chabon: Enterprise?

Silverblatt: Yes.
Chabon: That was one of the questions I really started with in working on this book. Doing the research, I very quickly got past Siegel and Shuster and began to notice that there was Joe Simon and Jack Kirby, whose original name was Jacob Kurtzberg. There was Bob Kane and Gil Kane, whose original name was Eli Katz. It was apparent to me that there were lots of young Jewish guys going in the comic book business in 1938, 1939, 1940, and I wanted to know why. I interviewed another great Jewish comic book creator, Will Eisner, creator of The Spirit, very early on in my work on this book, and I asked him about that. The first answer he gave me was kind of an economic answer. He said if you were a Jewish guy and you loved to draw and you wanted to make a living as an artist in the late 1930s, all the good paying fields were closed to you. They didn't hire Jews at the big advertising agencies. The only opportunity you had was comics. In fact, a lot of the comic companies were themselves owned by Jewish businessmen, so it was as simple as that. That's where you could get hired. But then he paused, and he said something that I actually ended up using as the epigraph for this book, which is that maybe there's something in Jewish culture, in Jewish folklore, in the received traditions of Jewish storytelling, that could produce a Superman or a Batman. Maybe we have this history of impossible solutions to insoluble problems—that there's a figure like the golem who can be made by a rabbi that will come to life and take revenge for the blood libels or who will protect the miserable dwellers of the Prague ghetto from oppressors. This avenger of the oppressed, this righter of wrongs, does possibly have some roots in that.

Silverblatt: When we last spoke, it was about *Wonder Boys*, and I had mentioned to you that an awful lot of activity circled around the locked trunk of the car in which all sorts of items, items that seemed to represent experiments that the id was performing, were at the center of the book. This book centers on an escape artist, and the liberation of libidinal energies is very much afoot here. But more important is the decision of the characters to be aware of these energies but not look very far into their source, and I wondered about that. In other words, the book sees the comic books as a substitute for personal exploration or wildness rather than an abettor of, or an invitation to.

Chabon: Right. To me, that's a possible definition of escapism. That's why "escapist literature" is such a powerful force. Speaking personally, I have always felt much more free in my imagination than in any other circumstance in my life. I'm at my best, at my freest, when I'm just sort of at play in my imagination, and the comic book [has the] ability to tap into that and to offer a kind of substitute for actually being able to do things oneself. I think most people go through life feeling, to one degree or another, like Houdini in a packing crate inside a canvas mailbag seventy feet under the River Seine. And most us are not escape artists; we don't have any actual physical means of self-liberation, and the only reliable way is through fantasy, through imagination, through mental play.

Silverblatt: The amazing thing about this book is that it is so performance-oriented. There's a lot of derring-do, swashbuckling, and mime, and triple-tiered climaxes arrive several times in the book, replete with ticking clocks. You're one of those rare cases of a really wonderful literary novelist who's at his best when entertaining, not when trying to bore into an interior. Why do you suppose that is, and do you agree?

Chabon: I don't have a whole lot of serious ambition for my work beyond trying to move and entertain a reader. I try to do that through faithful reporting of things as I see them or people as I see them, and through really pushing the English language to the degree that I am able. I don't want to use ordinary, common materials of entertainment, but I do want to entertain. I agree with you—I think the few times in my writing life when I've tried to write things, most of which have never seen the light of day, that were more polemical or more ruminative or speculative, or where I tried to articulate some kind of philosophy, my voice begins to ring falser and falser as I go farther and farther in that direction. But my only goal ever, really, is to try to write the kind of book that I think I would like to read—and I read for pleasure. Writers that don't bring me pleasure are writers that I don't read. That idea of bliss that Roland Barthes talks about—that's what I want to cause in a reader's mind.

Silverblatt: One of the things that I noticed while reading *Kavalier & Clay* is that the idea of escape contains in it two twin ideas: the idea of escaping *from* and the idea of escaping *to*. And it seemed to me that in this book, neither the escaped from nor the escaped to is of very much moment. Yes, because one of the heroes comes from Czechoslovakia and has a family there, there is a concern with escaping from fascism, but as others have noticed, it's a strangely lightweight kind—it's not the suffering of the entoiled masses. It's the kind of thing that a comic book does with fascism. And there's a character who, by the end of the book, is escaping to a world of his sexual promise, but that, too, remains relatively unembodied in the book. The characters don't have access in many ways to their past, they don't have access to their futures. And I found that to be characteristic, that your books have a very present-tense moment.

Chabon: Ultimately, the mystery of any feat of escape artistry is not seeing Houdini being wrapped up in chains and ropes and having the hood put over his head, and it's really not the moment when he steps out from behind the curtain dripping wet and free of all those chains and ropes. It's what's going on behind the curtain, the thing that we're not privy to. It's the actual work of escape itself, not the being chained, not the stepping out into the spotlight, but the actual labor, the secret work with the picks and the hidden key. I suppose in a sense that's kind of like the present to the past and future of the two halves of any escape act.

Silverblatt: Could you have written a book like *The Amazing Adventures of Kavalier & Clay* if you didn't begin by loving comics? Could you do this kind of book without the personal enthusiasm?

Chabon: I don't think so. I mean, it was a long haul. I spent four and a half years on this, and I don't think I would have had that kind of desire if there wasn't some sort of ancient core of my own personal imaginary life that I was tapping into. I had this box, the last box of my childhood comic book collection. I sold everything else and I kept this one box, and it followed me around for years, and I didn't open it for years. Then at some point soon after I finished writing *Wonder Boys*, I opened that box up. And the smell of moldering paper and the covers that I hadn't seen in years that I remembered perfectly—it was such a powerful sensory moment, and I knew there was something about that box of comics that I was going to be able to translate into a book. And if I didn't have that, then no. If I were interested in writing about the period of the 1930s and '40s in New York, I would have found some other way into the material, but that was one that I did have a personal stake in.

Silverblatt: You've now written three books—*The Mysteries of Pittsburgh*, *Wonder Boys*, and *The Amazing Adventures of Kavalier & Clay*—in which male bonding goes over into the territory of homosexuality and then withdraws from it—least so in *Wonder Boys*. But certainly in the first and third books, a lot of the emotive power comes from that decision. What draws you to that?

Chabon: There's something in the question of the roles that get assigned to people, whether one is straight or gay, and the sort of artificial boundaries that people have put up for them, or that people put up themselves, that is obviously a source of story for me. What I seem to keep coming back to is the idea of a friendship between a gay man and a straight man. In *The Mysteries of Pittsburgh*, it's Cleveland Arning and Arthur Lecomte, and in *Wonder Boys* you've got Crabtree and Grady Tripp, and then in this book, Sammy and Joe. To me, that's meaty. I like this idea that somehow there's a potential in the friendship—a real friendship, a bosom friendship—between a gay man and a straight man for the categories to get blurred, to get smudged. There's love between those two men, but what kind of love is it? You can't just say they're lovers, you can't just say they're buddies. There's something in between, there's this indefinite quantum state that you can't really pin down. There's an interesting tension there.

Silverblatt: Before the show I was talking to Art Spiegelman, a contemporary cartoonist, and we agreed that the most emotionally intense scene is the one at the closed World's Fair between Tracy Bacon and Sammy. They are making love to one another on the scene of a now-closed fair attraction—it's an aerial view of the entire city. It really is a scene that a romantic comedy would have had, even in their heyday, to work pretty hard to cook up as steamily as this. At the end, sparks are flying between these characters' fingers! And it does seem as if these books take, as a kind of center of their gravity, a choice between the imagination on the one hand, and sexual fulfillment on the other; straight or gay, the characters are given to enormous acts of self-abnegation. In the case of the heterosexual love in this book, the character runs away from his true love for a period of eight years. So, why is there this divide between the imagined life and the sexual one?

Chabon: I don't know. It's probably more apparent in retrospect or in reading than it is in the creation. Especially in the case of Sammy, it felt inevitable to me that, given the time he lived in and the kind of person he was, he would not be able to find any kind of fulfillment. There was this submerged sense of frustration in comic books from the very beginning—from the moment when Siegel and Shuster, these two nerdy, girlfriendless Cleveland kids, dream up this guy in blue tights that can fly around. There's an image of Jerry Siegel, the actual guy who really came up with Superman, lying in his bed on a hot summer night in Cleveland, just frustrated and bored and with a complete, crushing sense of his own insufficiency, just dreaming this up. It all comes to him in a flash, and he's kind of like the monk in that medieval woodcut poking his head through and seeing the machinery of the universe—and he's enlightened! He has this *satori* kind of moment, and it gets translated into this incredible thing called Superman.

My three-year-old son is running around the house in a Superman costume. There's power there. It's partly a sexual thing, it's partly a power thing, it's partly just the wish to be able to fly. It's a simple wish for total freedom, for being unfettered, in many more ways than simply sexually, that I think feeds into comics from the creation of the comic book to the domination of the comic book for a brief period in American history. Somehow the theme of frustration, of sublimation, of squelching one's desires, is just inevitably tied up in the counter-idea of being able to leap into the sky and fly away, free of all the forces of gravity and everything behind it, and being able to pick up a train car and throw it. It's not just power and it's not just sex—there's a fundamental enchainedness that everyone feels.

Silverblatt: It's a very interesting area. I remember talking to John Irving, who told me that he made the choice at a certain point to be an ordinary man with a schedule and an ordinary life. He said that the kinds of wildness that he found when he was younger and felt that life promised him, that he had to choose between that and the books—and he chose sublimation, and providing books that in a way titillate readers with all sorts of genderal edges and possibilities. There are probably more transsexuals roaming through John Irving's pages than in any other writer's. It begins to make me think that, when pursuing this vein in writing, it does end up being a matter of choice, to choose the . . .

Chabon: The box!

Silverblatt: The box.

Chabon: It is. Escape artistry is a metaphor for the writer's life in that every single day, you climb into that box. You're all alone; no one can help you. The only person who can get you out of the box is yourself. Plot is this horrible, nightmarish contraption once you begin to fasten it around yourself, once you climb into that water tank of plot where you've put all these forces in motion and you can't stop them. I think every writer must be able on some level to sympathize with Harry Houdini in that moment where it's all in your hands, you're the only one can do it, and there's no way out except by imagining a way out. What you're saying about John Irving sounds to me like you're describing Houdini climbing into a milk can. I think that sense of abnegation . . . I mean, plenty of people have made a comparison between their writer's life and the monastic life or life in the solitary cell, that kind of renunciation, but that metaphor doesn't really speak to me.

Silverblatt: No, because when they go into renunciation they're not supposed to think about the thing. But this is a withdrawal *in order* to think about the repressed and the impossible. It's almost like you sign a contract that says, "I will go there, but only as a visitor."

Chabon: In imagination. It's like the first line of Nabokov's *Pale Fire*, right? It's like the shadow of the waxwing slain, but in the false azure of the windowpane I've lived and flown on. I think that's where, in a way, writers spend their lives, in that false azure of the windowpane, where it's all in fancy, it's all in imagination.

Silverblatt: This brings something up, because we share a passion for Nabokov. In recent years, it has emerged that Nabokov's difficulty with his brother's more or less open homosexuality generated *Pale Fire*, but this was not something people dared to say when Nabokov was alive. In fact, Nabokov was quite a hectoring supervisor of his biographers, and he would become furious at biographers who said unsanctioned things that were accurate in the product of their research—they would be exiled to Siberia, they would have no further access.

Chabon: Or Zembla.

Silverblatt: [*laughter*] I would rather be in Zembla. But how do you feel about that place where the personal life secretly intersects with the life on the page?

Chabon: Well, that is the hub of everything, really. I understand why Nabo-

kov wanted to chase people away from that, not because of public embarrassment or personal embarrassment, but because that's the source of everything. The darkest, most frightening places, the things that you're most
afraid of, are exactly the things that you ought to be writing about. In Ger-
shom Scholem's essay on the idea of the golem, Scholem has this line that so
struck me. It's something like, "The act of creating a golem is an extremely
dangerous act to the creator." When I read that, it seemed like a perfect
metaphor for novel making. It's that autobiographical dance that the writer
does with the reader; the reader can't help flipping back to look at the author
photo to see if it matches the description of the character in any way. Or,
"Oh, it says here that he once lived in New Orleans, and this book's taking
place in New Orleans. I wonder if this could possibly be about him." That
doubt, that uncertainty, and the way that the writer plays with it, flirts with
it, draws upon it—I don't think you want people coming too close to that. If
that's a source of narrative for you, it's like an oracle. It's something that is
jealously guarded by a dragon.

Michael Chabon

Barbara Shoup and Margaret-Love Denman / 2000

From *Novel Ideas: Contemporary Authors Share the Creative Process*. Ed. Barbara Shoup and Margaret-Love Denman. 2001. 2nd edition. Athens: U of Georgia P, 2009. 115–26. Reprinted by permission.

Q: Your first novel, *The Mysteries of Pittsburgh*, was completed while you were working on your MFA. What was it like to work on a novel in a workshop setting? What kind of feedback did you get during the drafting process, and from whom?

A: I started writing a novel because I thought that everybody else at the UC Irvine workshop, when I got there, would be writing novels or would already have written novels. I began *Mysteries of Pittsburgh* out of self-defense, in other words. Of course when I arrived, with a hundred pages in tow, I found lots of people focusing exclusively on short stories and others whose first novels were still in the future.

I showed my hundred pages, soon after arrival at Irvine, to the great Oakley Hall, one of the two writer/professors then in charge of the program. He told me, essentially, with typical bluntness, "You have far too many characters and nowhere near enough story." And I saw at once that he was right. So I went back that afternoon and cut all but about fifteen pages, and spent the next week reconceiving the book much more in terms of two stories—the Art-Arthur-Phlox love triangle and the Art-Cleveland-father plot—committing myself at that point, without being sure how I would do it, to have the two stories intersect.

After that I turned the novel in to the workshop three times, roughly at one hundred pages, two hundred pages, and three hundred pages. The first time, the workshop was led by the other main Irvine guy, a man named Donald Heiney, since dead, who wrote some extremely interesting Steven Millhauser-ish novels under the pen name of MacDonald Harris. He be-

40

gan the workshop by saying, basically, "This is brilliant, it's wonderful, and clearly Michael knows what he's doing here. Anything any of us says to him beyond encouraging him to go on will only foul him up." So he essentially forbade any discussion. Needless to say, that rankled the other members of the workshop considerably. This came back to haunt me the next time I submitted it to the workshop—they were pretty well lying in wait! The third time, it was a finished manuscript, which I had already shown to Don Heiney. Without telling me, he had sent it to his agent in New York. A few weeks later, I got a call from Mary Evans, then at the Virginia Barber Literary Agency, saying they were going to take me on. So when the workshop started chopping it up the third time, I already knew that I had an agent who was pretty enthusiastic about her chances of selling it.

I don't want to give the impression that there was anything like a hostile environment in that workshop, by the way. We all got along very well, for the most part, socialized together a lot, et cetera, but they were an opinionated group and very articulate, and that first experience of being gagged by Don Heiney just sat very badly with them.

Q: Did you know that *Mysteries of Pittsburgh* was a novel right from the start, or did it start as a short story? If the latter, would you talk about how you came to realize that it was a novel? What is the difference between a short story and a novel, in your opinion?
A: I began the book with the conscious intention of writing a novel, which I tried to pattern loosely after my two favorite novels, *The Great Gatsby* and *Goodbye, Columbus* (which latter was, I believe, patterned to some degree on the former), in that it would take place over the course of a single summer.

A short story is a commando operation. It has a specific objective; you have to get in quickly, set your charges, and get out, leaving the reader to be caught up in the blast. A novel is more like a war: always begun in the highest enthusiasm, with full confidence of right, and of the certainty of it all being over by Christmas. Two years later you're in the trenches and the mud, with defeat a real possibility, doubting everything, in particular the wisdom of the commanding general.

Q: Would you describe the genesis of the novel and the process by which you found and wrote the story? What did you know when you began? What surprised you during the writing process?
A: All I knew when I began work was "I'm going to write a book about sum-

mer." What surprised me most, I suppose, was the realization, about two-thirds of the way through, that I was actually going to finish a novel!

Q: You had the experience that all novelists dream of having with a first novel—great reviews, great sales, comparisons to Dickens, Salinger, and F. Scott Fitzgerald. What was that like? In what ways was that kind of success not all a blessing? How do you think it shaped you as a developing writer?
A: It felt even less real as it was happening to me than it does now. And there were factors in my personal life, in my first marriage, that conspired to make every good thing that happened simultaneously a burden. I think that, in retrospect, that may have been a good thing. It was hard to feel too proud of myself. I'm not sure how it shaped me, although I think I have unquestionably benefited from having the sense, after *Mysteries*, of there being a real audience for my writing, small but loyal—I mean my gay readers. They have always been there for me and I have taken a lot of heart over the years from knowing they were there.

Q: Though *Wonder Boys* is your second published novel, it is not the second novel you wrote. Would you describe that second novel—what you were attempting with it, why it was so difficult, and what ultimately happened to it?
A: I feel as I've talked about this book so much by now that perhaps I ought just to have published it and thereafter shut up! It was a novel called *Fountain City* and was primarily concerned with the attempt by a developer, an architect, and his apprentice, to build the perfect baseball park on the Gulf Coast of Florida. But there were lots of subplots and sub-subplots dealing with Paris, French cooking, environmentalism, and a plot to rebuild the Temple in Jerusalem. I think I started out telling a fairly simple story about an architect who lived in a kind of classical dreamworld and then [I] got more and more reckless in adding ingredients to the brew . . . just tossing in all kinds of stuff I was (and remain) interested in, and trusting—wrongly, as it turned out—that it would come out not merely edible but tasty and nourishing.

Q: For many novelists, the second novel is actually more difficult to write than the first. Why do you think this is so?
A: I don't know; it took me twenty-two years to write my first novel, but only seven to finish a second, and four for this latest one—maybe it's getting easier!

Q: What was the genesis of *Wonder Boys*? Would you talk about the process by which you found and wrote that story? What did you know when you began, and what surprised you?

A: I was terrified by the ongoing failure of *Fountain City*. Five and a half years into it, I began to worry that I would never finish it, that I would keep on writing it for the rest of my life. I didn't think I had the guts to walk away. But then one day my then fiancée, now wife, announced to me that she was going to take the California Bar Exam six months earlier than she originally had intended. Which meant that between studying and her job as a clerk for a federal district judge, she would be completely unavailable to me for the next six weeks.

It was like a bolt of lightning. Something inside me said, "Now's your chance." I went down to my office under our house in San Francisco, opened a new file, and just started writing. I wrote the first five or seven pages in a night, pretty much as they are in the final book, and just kept on going. It was very strange; I have no idea where any of it came from, beyond my apparent desire to create, in Grady Tripp, a writer who had screwed himself even more than I had. It was as if, once I had made the decision to use this six-week period to "cheat on" *Fountain City*, some story-telling part of my consciousness was liberated. Seven months later I had a solid first draft.

Q: Did you imagine the scene in which Grady Tripp's novel blows away when you conceived of your novel, or was it something that came to you in the process of writing it?

A: I think that episode pretty much arose out of the moment. I didn't really know until I got there what was going to happen to Grady's manuscript, to his work on the novel.

Q: Was James Leer based in any way on yourself and your own experiences as a young writer, or on the experiences of someone you know? Do other characters in the book have counterparts in real people?

A: James Leer was sort of an amalgam of me and a couple other "boy genius" writers I had known in school, and I use the quotes advisedly. And real people usually manage to work their way into all of my characters, somehow or other.

Q: *Wonder Boys* is hilarious, but also powerful because it is true on the most fundamental level. Any writer who has been through an MFA program or even just attended a writers' conference recognizes the basic truth in your depiction of that world. To what degree do you think that the work of a serious novelist is helped and/or hindered either as a teacher or student, in these programs? Can writing be taught? For you, what is the benefit of having earned the MFA degree?

A: It really all depends on the program, which in turn depends on (1) most importantly, the amount of financial support the program offers to students, so that they can concentrate on their writing; (2) the quality and commitment to teaching of the faculty; and (3) the tone of the workshop itself, which grows in part out of (2) and in part from the nature of the students. If you get yourself into a program that supports you both emotionally and financially, with teachers who inspire by example and help you past some of the shoals and rocks that confront the young writer, then you can really blossom.

Q: What is talent, in your opinion? How does it fit into the mix?

A: Talent is, with luck, one of the two out of three required elements for success, both artistic and material, as a writer, over which the writer has absolutely no control, and for which he or she can take no credit at all. The third absolutely required element, and the only one the writer can both ensure and take pride in, is discipline.

My view of talent is like that of the catcher Crash Davis in *Bull Durham*, when he's lecturing Nuke LaLoosh on the importance of discipline in pitching: "God reached down and turned your right arm into a thunderbolt. It has nothing to do with you." Literary talent is an accident of birth, like the ability to spot four-leaf clovers, and about as meaningful in the absence of hard work.

Q: Your novels have become longer and more complex; each one is a completely different kind of story, yet certain things show up again and again. Would you comment on the idea of a writer's material? Where does it come from? How do you recognize an idea as your own? In what ways does your own material reflect the experiences that shaped you as a child?

A: That's what Henry James called "the figure in the carpet." It's a kind of an inherent signature—a watermark—that can be seen in every work by a particular writer when you hold it up to the light. I'm sure that the explanations lie in my childhood and adolescence as a lonely, dreamy, socially outcast child of divorce, but beyond that I prefer not to think about it too much, to be honest. I'm just glad to know it's there.

My ideas are just . . . my ideas. I've never had one that I didn't like, that didn't just seem to arise bearing the promise of being very interesting—to me.

Q: *The Amazing Adventures of Kavalier & Clay* moves into the heads of characters who seem purely invented and who live in a completely different time. Where did the idea for this book come from? How did it develop? How is the book you wrote the same as and different from the book you imagined at the start?

A: This book ultimately grew out of an ongoing conversation between me and my father, all through my childhood, about the world of his childhood, in Brooklyn, which he remembered in deep and fond detail. The comic books, the movies, the radio programs, the political and social history, the music, the games, and landscape of his boyhood; he brought them to vivid life in my imagination. I guess I just wanted to do the same thing for readers. From the start I knew that I wanted to try to cover the entire period of the so-called Golden Age of Comic Books, circa 1938–1954.

It's funny. When I finished the book, I felt that I had really wandered very far from my original ideas about what kind of a book it would be. That I had made all kinds of surprising discoveries and decisions along the way that I never could have foreseen. And then I came across a brief note I had written to myself, four and a half years earlier, as I prepared to start to work. In this note I laid out my intentions for the book and for what I thought it would be like, what kind of territory it would cover. And it was remarkably like the final draft! I was amazed.

Q: Creating the character of The Escapist, Sammy asks Joe, "What is the why?" This seems to be fundamental to creating characters that are believable and compelling. Would you talk about this idea in terms of how you go about creating the characters in your novels?

A: I guess I'll just say that when I get into trouble working on a book, it's almost always because I don't understand my character or characters' motivations; there's a disjunction between the behavior of the character as dictated by the needs of my plot and what he or she really would do in the situation, whatever the situation is. And until I sort out and get a very firm grip on "the why," I can't really proceed.

Q: How do your characters most often show themselves to you in the beginning stages of writing a novel? How do they clarify and begin to shape the action of it?

A: It depends. Some characters come together, from their aches and the sources of those aches down to their smallest particulars of speech and dress, very quickly and effortlessly. And once I have a good sense of them, I can sort of sit back and let them do what they do. Other characters go through endless permutations and revisions, turning from wicked to kind to whimsical to mad and back again, and I'll struggle from draft to draft to draft to get to the heart of the character and to what his or her function in the book must be. In this latter case, sometimes the problem character will just one day abruptly pop into place, and I'll say, "Oh, of course!" And sometimes he or she never comes together, and I just have to cut him or her out.

Q: You gave the reader the "why" of the comic book character Tom Mayflower in a separate chapter early in the book. Later, Judy Dark's "why" was given a chapter. In each case, the stories are in large part woven of issues and memories that their creators are grappling with at the moment of creation, and real-world details that they encounter going about their day-to-day lives while the story is percolating on an unconscious level. Would you talk about how these chapters describe the process by which the novel itself was made? What issues, questions, memories, and details of your real life made their way into the fabric of the story during the process of writing it?
A: This is a very good question, but unfortunately I don't think I can give it a very good answer. It's such an intuitive process that for the most part I'm not even aware that it's happening, and often it won't be until later, when somebody points it out to me, that I see how much of some real-life experience or concern of mine has been reconfigured in the fiction. And yet, as the examples you give suggest, it's a process that I'm fully aware of, that, in fact, I rely on.

My life, my memories and desires, are the bits of string, colored paper, yarn, tinfoil, et cetera—not particularly interesting in themselves—that I assemble into the collages of my novels and stories.

Q: The practice of magic is a thread that runs through the book. Would you discuss the ways in which you think magic is a metaphor for the process of writing a novel? What rules of magic apply to creating a novel?
A: The magic, to me, is in the enjoyment of a work of art, not in the creation of it. In other words, the novelist has not performed any magic at all until his or her book is in a reader's hands, is reaching directly into that reader's mind and is transporting the reader out of his or her own soul, the suffering and tedium of the reader's quotidian life. Everything up to that point is craft.

Q: In *The Amazing Adventures of Kavalier & Clay*, you regularly introduced new elements, building on what had come before to torque the tension of the novel. How did you create the plot of the novel? Which twists and turns of the plot did you know at the outset and which ones revealed themselves as you wrote? How did you keep all the various strands of the book straight, both in your head and on the page?

A: It was pretty much a long, often painful and dull process of trial and error, groping my way along, writing and rejecting long passages that went nowhere. I subscribe to the perdition theory of plotting: you just have to get very, very lost, a lot. I know very little, when I'm starting out, about the plot, and in fact a lot of things I think I know end up getting discarded because they turned out to be not germane or simply superfluous.

But at a certain point I will begin to get caught up in the story myself, almost the way a reader does, and the things that happen next will have this marvelous sense of inevitability. And then, as I'm closing in on the end of the first draft, I will sit down and plot out the last part of the book. After that, I try to figure out where I'm going. Before I begin the next draft, I make a very thorough outline. At this point, for the first time, I start to question myself about the dominant motifs of the book, the themes that seem to be emerging, and I try to use the answers to these questions to help guide the plot choices I make, discarding elements and episodes that seem beside the point, and trying to forge new links for the chain, tempered by my deeper understanding of what it is I seem to be trying to say.

But I'm making the process of revision outlining sound much more articulate and drawn out than it really is. It's really a matter of about a half-hour's work, and my notes to myself are very fragmentary, and later often turn out to be not especially helpful.

Q: Would you describe the research you did for *Kavalier & Clay*? Did you do most of the research before you began writing, or as you wrote? What rules did you set for yourself in your use of the real people, like Salvadore Dalí and Al Smith, who appear in the book?

A: I did a lot of library research, poring over old back issues of the *New Yorker*, going through back issues of the *New York Times* on microfilm. I read histories of comic books, histories of America during the period. I spend a month in New York, doing research at the New York Historical Society library—especially looking through their collections of old photos of the city. And I had the 1939 *WPA Guide to New York City*, which I carried around, trying to see the city as it was then. I interviewed a lot of surviving Golden

Age comics creators, trying to jog their memories of the time. And then as I wrote, subjects kept working their way into the book that obliged me to go back to the library: the Antarctic, Houdini, the Empire State Building, the golem.

I had some reservations about using "celebrity characters." It's a widely [used], perhaps overused fictional "trick" nowadays. But ultimately I decided since these people—Dalí, Al Smith, Orson Welles—kept cropping up in my research, over and over, they were a legitimate part of the cultural landscape of the time, as much as the smoke-ring-blowing Camel sign in Times Square, and that it would be not only silly but mistaken to leave them out. So my rule was just not to let them be anything more than minor characters, taking cameo roles. I kept them in the background.

Q: A number of things in the book either mirror or are reminiscent of real events of that time. For example, Hans Hoffman's failed effort to bring the Jewish children to America on *The Ark of Miriam* echoes the incident in which a shipful of Jewish children reached America, but were turned away at immigration. How did these real things work their way into the book? In what ways did your research discoveries shape character and/or plot? In what ways did you transform real events to suit the needs of the story?
A: The research really did drive the plot. For example, I was reading about comic books in a magazine devoted to older, "vintage" comics, and there happened to be an article about the 1960s comics artist named Jim Steranko who had had an earlier career as an escape artist. When I read that, a light just came on. The idea of escape just felt instantly right, though I wasn't really sure, yet, why.

That was an experience that got repeated over and over again: some little tidbit in my reading would just ring a bell, and the shape of the book, the destinies of the characters, would change.

Q: Why did you decide to use the occasional footnotes throughout the book?
A: I was trying to confuse the reader. I wanted him or her to have moments of very serious uncertainty about just how fictional this book, and in particular the characters of Kavalier and Clay, really were. Footnotes are a weirdly effective way of lending an aura of fact to your lies.

Q: What were the pleasures and perils of research for you?
A: It was pretty much all pleasure to immerse myself in the history, images,

and atmosphere of this era that had always meant so much to me. The peril was, first of all, that it was always more fun to go to the library and read old *New Yorker*s than to write; and, second, that doing too much research sometimes started to make me feel imprisoned by the facts. There always comes a point when you have to put research aside and just start making shit up.

Q: What is your process of revision? Do people read for you? If so, what kind of feedback do you depend on them to give you?
A: I revise as I go along, and then from draft to draft. Generally, I begin each night's writing session by going over what I did the night before. My principal techniques for identifying the parts that need work are (1) listening carefully to the sound of the words with my "inner ear"—I can usually hear the wonky parts; and (2) attending to the feeling in my gut: a clenching, uneasy, anxious clutch of dissatisfaction that seems to bloom whenever I'm reading my way through a weak section.

My wife is always my first reader, and over the years I have trained her to be harsh in her judgments. And for this latest book I gave drafts to a lot of people, far more than had been my practice in the past. I think I was worried more about this book than about previous ones—it was so big and complicated, and plus there was the whole period element. And I got some very helpful readings. It was like being back in workshop again. I think I'll probably do the same thing with the next book.

Q: Have you ever experienced writer's block? What is writer's block, in your opinion?
A: No. Like Grady Tripp, I don't believe in writer's block. If you're disciplined about your work—meaning you do it at the same time every day, for the same amount of time—you'll have bad days at the keyboard, days when you struggle and it all comes out crap. But it will come out, because you will have trained your writing organ to wake up when your butt hits the chair.

Q: After living intensely in the world of *Kavalier & Clay*, what was it like to finish the book and think about moving on to another set of characters, another world? Would you talk about what it's like to live in a novel—how it impinges on your real life, how your real life funnels into it?
A: I was mostly just relieved by the time I finished the book. There was a little bit of sadness, because it had been a pleasurable experience, and I knew I was never going to have quite the same relationship again to Glenn Miller's

music, Jack Benny, Eleanor Roosevelt, et cetera, that I had felt while writing the book. I was back in my own time again, for the foreseeable future. But mostly I was just relieved.

Q: What is it like to let go of a book and send it into the world of readers and reviewers? Would you talk about how you deal with the business end of being a successful novelist?

A: It's an extremely anxious time. And again, as the reviews come in and are, hopefully, mostly good, what I feel is largely relief. But it's very exciting and wondrous to hear from readers, to hear what they liked in the book, what made them laugh or cry, what their favorite sentences are. I deal with the business end of being a novelist by trusting in my agent, Mary Evans. And so far this has proven to be a very wise policy.

Fissionable Material:
An Interview with Michael Chabon

Neil Gaiman / 2003

From *Ruminator Review* 13 (Spring 2003): 26–28, 50. © Neil Gaiman. Reprinted by permission.

One of the most welcome recent trends in the publishing business has been the blurring of the line between "serious" literary novels and genre fiction—suddenly, writers once read only by small groups of dedicated genre fans are breaking into the mainstream, and authors known for their high-minded work are using elements of everything from ghost stories to *Superman.*

Perhaps no two writers represent this trend in more ways, and from more angles, than Michael Chabon and Neil Gaiman. Since his debut with *The Mysteries of Pittsburgh* in 1988, Chabon has been classified among the rising stars of contemporary literary fiction. *Wonder Boys,* his 1995 novel about a professor in the throes of a midlife crisis, proved a commercial and critical success. In 2001, Chabon took home the Pulitzer Prize for fiction with *The Amazing Adventures of Kavalier & Clay,* his genre-bending look at the history of 1940s and '50s America through the eyes of two young comic book creators in that medium's golden age. Chabon's most recent book—and first for young readers—is *Summerland,* an adventure novel based on equal parts American myth and world-crossing fantasy.

Gaiman is also relatively new to the children's literature world, having published his second young adult book, *Coraline,* in 2002. His name is most familiar, however, to fans of contemporary comics and science fiction. Gaiman is best known as the creator and writer of the dark, erudite, and mythologically savvy *Sandman* series, a best-selling touchstone of the 1990s alternative-comics movement. He's also written for stage, radio, film, and television, where he created the BBC miniseries *Neverwhere* based on his novel. In 2001, Gaiman found his greatest mainstream literary success with *American Gods*, a biting satire that places traditional Norse gods square in the middle of the contemporary United States, with illuminating results.

Chabon and Gaiman sat down together in February at the University of Minnesota to discuss myth, genre, contemporary literature, and a host of other topics. Thanks to the Esther Freier Endowment and the Department of English at the University of Minnesota for bringing Mr. Chabon to town. Special thanks to Mary Ellis and Lorriane Garland for working out the logistics.

Gaiman: Was there any temptation to start collecting comics when you were writing *The Amazing Adventures of Kavalier & Clay*?
Chabon: Yeah, and I did. When I was a kid I had a couple thousand comic books. I sold them when I got interested in rock and roll music and took that money to buy records and a good stereo. I held on to my Jack Kirby comic books because he was my favorite. I have a pretty extensive library as a result of *Kavalier & Clay*—not just comics but comics history, graphic novels, and bound archive editions of classic, golden age comics.

Gaiman: It feels like with *Kavalier & Clay* you entered a new phase as a writer. It's not more confident, because you had this amazing sort of cocky confidence from *The Mysteries of Pittsburgh* on, but it seems like much more of a readiness to go wherever your muse takes you.
Chabon: I think that's true. I think I learned that about myself in writing *Kavalier & Clay*. It wasn't that I thought this was going to be the one where I really pulled out all the stops, but I started to feel that if something crossed my mind and my first thought was, I can't do that, then my second thought would be, yes, I can do that. Maybe it was partly that my subject matter was comic books, maybe that gave me a certain sense of freedom. The material I was working with had such strong elements of the fantastic. I thought, I can't do this justice if I treat it with calipers and tongs and keep it at arm's length. If this material is coming out of a place where imagination is un- bridled and boundless, where guys can fly through the air and shoot flames out of their hands, then instead of keeping it safe between panes of glass as if I were observing fissionable material, I thought that I would just get into it. I'll let all those fantasy isotopes come through and contaminate the material I'm writing. As soon as I started doing that it felt really good. Not only that, but I guess I knew I could do it, that I was up to it and I felt capable of it.

Gaiman: There is a wonderful moment in *Kavalier & Clay*—there are a huge number of marvelous moments—that touched me personally on a very odd level. You're describing the strange, flush, sleepless weekend of creation when the young writers and artists are coming up with all these new comic book characters.

Chabon: Absolutely. That's part of the joy for me of that period of comic book history. The market was so explosive just then. Everyone was jumping on the comics bandwagon. There were so many publishers churning out so much material for this brief period that they would try anything. It was like a moment in evolution when nature seems to run rampant, spawning all kinds of forms and mutations. Many of them turn out to be dead ends, but there are these incredible periods where it's just uncontrolled permutation of a few simple elements. All of these characters had tight costumes, boots, a mask, and some kind of power that exceeds ordinary human power. Obviously you're going to have lots of dross when something like that's going on, but what I really liked was just that sense of unlimited recombination and permutation. You had characters like Hydroman, who could turn into water. What possible use is that? That he could make himself a puddle on the ground so that a criminal would slip when he was running past. Hydroman had the most ridiculous power, but he lasted for a couple of years, I think.

Gaiman: Is theme something that you find at the beginning of writing a book, or something that you see looking back?

Chabon: It emerges in the course of the writing. When I start writing, it's almost always with a very rudimentary sense of character, setting, the general action of the story. With *Kavalier & Clay* I had this idea of a tall, thin guy and a little, short guy, and they were going to be a team cut out of the same cloth as Don Quixote and Sancho Panza in some way. I knew I wanted to cover the golden age of comics in New York during the Second World War, from the creation of Superman to the book by Fredric Wertham, *Seduction of the Innocent*, which spawned the senate subcommittee hearings of 1954 [on the supposedly evil effects of comics on children]. That was my last time frame. I had these vague ideas, and I'd just start writing. The things that became the themes of the book emerged through the writing: the idea of escape, the idea of the golem, of the magical collaboration that brings a being to life but then takes on a life of its own that the creators never imagined. Those things emerged out of the story very organically.

Often I finish a whole first draft without having given the question of theme a moment's thought. It's not until I look at that first draft and feel lost that I ask myself, what is this book really about? Why do I have these characters? What's this woman doing in this story? She's interesting, but she's not doing anything. How can I use her effectively? For example, the comic book hero that Sammy and Joe created in *Kavalier & Clay* was originally just a generic strongman character. It took my sitting down with a draft and saying, I have this thing about escaping from Prague, and I have this element of escapist literature. Just at the moment when I was wrestling with thematic questions for the book, I stumbled on a magazine article about Jim Steranko's career as an escape artist and I just thought, escape artistry, escapism—this is clearly a theme I'm working with here. I went back and introduced the whole idea of Joe Kavalier's having trained to be an escape artist in Prague. It became very clear to me that the character Sammy and Joe created was going to be a superpowered escape artist, a super-Houdini character. All of a sudden I had a thematic element. Theme isn't something you start with or put in. It isn't just because there's some rule saying that you need to have themes in literature; theme is always, fundamentally, something that helps you tell your story.

Gaiman: It's that weird thing that's almost inexpressible—what is the story about? It's not actually plot. You can call it theme or whatever, but that's not necessarily what it's about. Sometimes you only find it after three different drafts.

Chabon: If you're thinking thematically to begin with, you're killing the language, you're killing the characters. But at a certain point you have to switch over to viewing your story the way a reader would view it, the way you were trained to read in school, to look for symbolism and theme and pattern of metaphor.

Gaiman: If we're doing our job, one of the things that you always know when you're stuck in a story is that you've written the answer in there somewhere anyway. You've set up a solution, and it always takes less work to fix it than you think.

Chabon: Exactly. I showed my first draft of *The Mysteries of Pittsburgh* to my teacher Oakley Hall at the University of California at Irvine. It wasn't even a finished first draft—110 pages. It was nothing but all these young people meeting each other and deciding whether to go to bed or not. It was very episodic and not very interesting. I knew that. I had reached the point of asking, what am I doing? Why do I think I want to write this story?

What's this about? Why am I talking about this young man in particular? My teacher gave me severe criticism: "This is just episodic and repetitive." Then he turned to page 6, a passage about the metallic groan produced by my father's recliner chair when he hurled his gangster body into it. My teacher asked: "What do you mean by 'gangster body' there? Is he a gangster?" And I said: "No. He just has a big, Luca Brasi kind of build." And he said, "Oh."

There was something about the way he said "Oh," the disappointment in his voice, and I thought, what if he *is* a gangster? It just started to click for me. Suddenly my main character came much more sharply into focus as the son of this guy with mob connections. I had sort of planted that word there, *gangster,* and I hadn't noticed it. It took someone else pointing it out to me and showing me that it was there, asking to be used, to be developed.

I think it's important to show your work to other people and to have readers that you trust to help you find things that you might be completely unaware of. You've laid pipe for something that you're not using and it's going to waste.

Gaiman: My only rule on that is that when they tell you there's something wrong, they're always right. But when they say what it is, they're almost always wrong.

Chabon: That's a great rule. The mark of a good reader to me is simply that he or she can locate the zones of trouble. It's almost never useful to have somebody make a specific suggestion. What you need is someone who will say, "I started to feel there's too much about the strawberry picking in this section." And what turns out is that there's not enough about the strawberry picking thing, and you need to go way deep into the whole world of strawberry picking and that's just what the book needs. But the problem was right where your reader was pointing—that's where things started to go wrong.

Gaiman: Let's talk about the issue of *McSweeney's* on genre writing that you're editing.

Chabon: To me what it's really about is my feelings about the short story. It all started because as a writer of short stories, I reached a point where I was feeling really trapped, constrained by my understanding, which admittedly might be flawed, of what a short story could be now, in this era, in the history of the short story. I was writing the same kind of story over and over again. I think I was getting better at it in some ways. But there's often a slenderness about the contemporary short story. It's intensely psychological, it's about characters and their emotions, about a tiny shift, even, in the way someone's looking at something in his or her life. Fantastic, lasting, beautiful work has been done within the genre of the short story, but I just started to think, is this all that we can do?

I went back to the anthologies on my shelf, books with titles like *Twenty Great Short Stories* or *Fifteen Classic Tales* of this or that. And looking through them I noticed two things right away. A lot of them were what we would now call genre stories: ghost stories, western stories, war stories, horror stories, suspense stories. Then I noticed that a lot of these genre stories were written by people like Edith Wharton, Henry James, Joseph Conrad, and Somerset Maugham. Apparently, there didn't used to be as strict a ghettoization of the genres of literature as there is now. And maybe because of that, writers whom we now consider to be serious literary writers were free to write in any genre they felt like. If a writer like Joseph Conrad wanted to write a spy story, he wrote a spy story. He didn't have to apologize for it, and it wasn't viewed as being extra-literary.

That started me thinking about what happened to all those other kinds of short stories. We still have a few science fiction magazines and maybe even a mystery magazine left—I'm not even sure if *Ellery Queen* is still published. The market for short genre fiction dried up. But, weirdly, genre novels are alive and well. The science fiction novel's alive and well; the mystery novel's alive and well. We have writers who have even managed to achieve a literary reputation working more or less within the traditional genre, or you have some like, say, Elmore Leonard, who is widely regarded as a fine American writer, one who happens to write crime stories and so on. But he doesn't write a whole lot of short stories. Why not?

So I started thinking, what can I do? One thing I can do is to write my own genre short stories, so I've been trying my hand. I've written a couple of horror stories. I just finished a novella that's actually a Sherlock Holmes story. I'm trying in my own work to incorporate some of the more traditional short story genres into my personal understanding of the short story.

But then I thought, what if I could get other people to do that? Especially people who write genre novels, but not short stories because there's just not much opportunity or market for them to do it. They can't make a living at all. Or what about people who write literary "short stories" but haven't ever tried writing a ghost story, someone like Rick Moody, for example? What would happen if he got an invitation to do it? What if we could publish this work in a context where the writers weren't going to feel ghettoized by doing it? Maybe there would be a way to slip past people with this material without their being alerted by the little atom symbol on the spine or the unicorn symbol that this is a work of science fiction or fantasy, which somehow automatically triggers a gag reaction with people who ought to know better.

And the neat thing is that a lot of the writers who participated—people like Chris Offutt, Rick Moody, and Sherman Alexie—said they were having the most fun they've had writing in years. Sherman Alexie e-mailed me to say, "I can't believe I never tried this before. What was my problem?" That's how I felt, too. There's a whole set of tools we're not using.

Someday I'd like to have a magazine, and if I ever do, I'm going to publish genre fiction, short stories by the best writers—whether they're commonly recognized as being genre writers or not. I'm not going to make any distinctions like that. The only thing will be that the work has to be truly a work of genre fiction and that it can't be winking or ironic or condescending. I'm not interested in pastiche.

The whole purpose is to make fiction better, broader, more all-encompassing than it is right now. Short fiction in particular.

Gaiman: I've always been pretty lucky in that I started off resolutely in the gutter and have done my very best to remain there despite people's attempts to drag me out. But one of the things that fascinate me is that it always seemed the most interesting literary stuff was happening in the places of confluence. You'd see all of these streams coming together—
Chabon: And enlarging.

Gaiman: I worry that we're cutting ourselves off from our roots.
Chabon: I agree. The roots of story-telling lie deep in traditions of the fantastic, the speculative, the ghost story, the tale. I think the novel overall, at least in English, has done better at holding on to those traditional, underlying elements. The novel weathered modernism with more of its past intact than the short story did. Modernism had a scouring effect on the short story, as it did on so many other arts—music and painting and so on. In a way, the short story never quite recovered.

The pulps helped begin the ghettoization of genres. Because they were cheap, and serious people didn't read them. Then, when the more literary kind of short story magazines began to die out, I think that was the end. *Collier's* and *Liberty* and the *Saturday Evening Post*. The *New Yorker*'s still around, although they used to publish two stories a week and now they publish one. In the glory days of the "slicks" you had stories like Stephen Vincent Benét's "By the Waters of Babylon," an early postapocalypse story. This was a very key kind of story, I think, in helping a lot of people imagine the world after some kind of unnamed disaster, probably from the early 1920s, published, I think, in the *Saturday Evening Post.*

Gaiman: Shirley Jackson's "The Lottery," which probably got picked up and reprinted in things like *Galaxy* but made its first appearance, I think, in the *New Yorker* to a storm of protest from people who hadn't quite understood that it was fiction. They thought it was chronicling some out-of-the-way American custom.

Chabon: And she suffered from the effects of that ghettoization thereafter. If you wrote "The Lottery" now, it would be hard to find a place to publish it simply because people would say, "Well, we just don't publish that sort of thing." Which is very unfortunate. What made Jorge Luis Borges so startling and interesting was the way in which what he was doing could be seen as science fiction or it could be seen as fantasy or it could be seen as horror. He was unashamedly trolling the waters of science fiction and fantasy but doing something that nobody had ever done before.

Gaiman: One of the things I discovered while doing *Coraline,* a children's book, was suddenly realizing you're not allowed to be in more than one ghetto at a time. If you're already in the kiddie lit ghetto, you're on the shelf next to historicals, science fiction, urban angst novels about eleven-year-old heroin addicts, next to 1930s adventure.

Chabon: And that's really the way it should be, in my opinion, with all fiction. The distinctions that can be made are between quality and the lack thereof. A great novel in science fiction ought to be just as great as a great novel about couples divorcing in suburban Connecticut or whatever.

Gaiman: I tend to think of all the different techniques as tools—you grab the right tool for the job and you come back up and that's what you use to write.

Chabon: Exactly. Why limit yourself? It's crazy. Especially crazy to do it because other people are telling you you have to. Whether it's the people who decide what section of the bookstore your books are going to go in or whether it's publishers or editors—those people have a lot of power and authority, but you don't want them telling you what to write.

Gaiman: Again, I was lucky in comics. Comics is a medium that gets mistaken for a genre, which meant that I got to spend my twenties and thirties splashing around in every genre I wanted to write in with nobody noticing because I was already in comics.

Chabon: People who are writing what they think of as "serious literary fiction"—and I'm always putting that in quotation marks—are almost self-policing, self-censoring in a way that well-behaved children often tend to be.

Gaiman: Part of the joy of genre is you need to understand that there are rules, and then you can start to break them. I always feel that blank verse should only be written by people who've actually learned how to write sonnets, sestinas, and villanelles first for two or three years and say, "OK. Now you know all that stuff. Now go write free verse."

Chabon: *Moby-Dick* is a genre novel. People tend to think that Herman Melville first wrote popular, successful accounts of his whaling voyages and then wrote this massive, magnificent novel, the serious literary novel that just happens to be about a whaling expedition but is really about relationships between God and man and man's place in the universe and so on and so forth. Well, no. *Moby-Dick* is just another whaling story, it's a sea story. *Huckleberry Finn* is a genre novel. And that's part of what makes it so great.

Gaiman: I read a wonderful essay recently about Henry James's story *The Turn of the Screw*. The essayist could not admit that it was a ghost story. Therefore, the only legitimate reading James could possibly have intended was that this was a story about madness.

Chabon: Absolutely. Everything in that story tells you how to read it: it's Christmas and at Christmastime in England they sit around and tell ghost stories. I think what makes the story so great is that it admits to multiple interpretations very deliberately—you could see the character as mad or you could read it as a ghost story if you want to. It's not limiting itself in the way that a much more straightforward story, say a Sheridan Le Fanu ghost story, might limit itself to just being a ghost story. Maybe because he's a great artist, Henry James is able to have it both ways.

Gaiman: What are you working on now?

Chabon: I'm writing a novel that's set in a Yiddish-speaking country in lower Alaska that was settled by refugees from Europe during the Second World War.

Gaiman: So, it's an alternate history?

Chabon: It's about a couple of policemen, so there's a mystery—but it's set in an alternate world where Israel never happened. There was this other outlet for the refugees from Europe.

Gaiman: Somebody was telling me that in real life there was an alternate plan for a Jewish settlement somewhere like Tanganyika.
Chabon: Uganda. That was a British plan. It got very close, and then the Balfour Declaration came around and the British laid aside the Uganda plans in favor of Palestine. There was talk about putting Jews in Madagascar, Surinam, a number of other parts. And then of course in the early nineteenth century there was the great Mordecai Noah here in the United States who had bought an island near Buffalo, New York. He wanted all the Jews in the world to come live on Grand Island. But that came to nothing. Ben Katchor did a brilliant comic called *The Jew of New York* that involves the Mordecai Noah story.

Gaiman: That was a wonderful comic.
Chabon: Yeah. I think it's one of the best in the past five or ten years.

Gaiman: So why Alaska?
Chabon: I got interested in this possibility. Actually, the novel came out of an essay I wrote. The essay was about *Say It in Yiddish: A Phrasebook for Travelers*. It's part of a series, the *Say It In* books. There's *Say It in Swahili*, and *Say It in German* and *Say It in French*. I loved the Yiddish book, partly because it's incredibly hilarious. There are all these great phrasebook kinds of phrases like, "Excuse me. Where can I find a tourniquet?" It's funny from that perspective.

But even more than that, it raises the question of where you could possibly go with a Yiddish phrasebook for travelers. I found a lot of sadness in the fact that there is no such country. In this essay I talk about how it was not out of the question that they might have decided to choose Yiddish as the language of Israel, but they didn't. Then I mentioned in passing that there was a plan to settle the Jews of Europe in Alaska that was briefly discussed during the Second World War—Franklin Roosevelt entertained this idea. Then I started to imagine what that country might have been like.

Then finally, of course, there was the idea that if Hitler hadn't happened, there would presumably be lots of Yiddish-speaking Jews in Europe. There would still be cities like Lublin, Poland, whose population was forty to fifty percent Jews. The idea of a Yiddish-speaking element of contemporary Europe was the conclusion of the essay.

But I started thinking about this territory in Alaska and the idea of what if there had never been an Israel and if there was this other kind of a Jewish country in the world, one that would be very different because of climate, location, history or the lack thereof, language, culture, all of those things. The more I tried to imagine what that country would be like and how the world would be a different place, the more I found that I couldn't get it out of my mind.

Gaiman: I remember reading an essay at some point about classic science fiction. The author suggested that there are three kinds: "What if?," "If only," and "If this goes on." I find that that's true for pretty much all fiction. Your new novel—is it a "What if?" or an "If only"?

Chabon: I guess it takes the form of a "What if?," but I think underlying it, at its heart, is "If only." To me Ashkenazic, Jewish, primarily Yiddish-speaking culture was an incredibly rich culture that was just beginning to come into its own, had just started to produce writers like Isaac Bashevis Singer and his older brother, Joshua. It had its Mark Twain in Sholem Aleichem, and it was in a way—aside from the fact that American literature had all of the English literature behind it—at a very similar stage of development to American literature. Then in the forties it was completely cut short and destroyed. All that really survives of that culture are people like us—non-Yiddish-speaking children and grandchildren and great-grandchildren. There are fragments of it here and there that continue to survive. But the immense tragedy of that loss haunts me.

I can't help thinking that it might have been a wonderful thing for there to be such a place as I'm trying to imagine in this book. By contrast, Israel—leaving aside all the incredible political complications and the historical questions and legitimacy and just looking at it as a cultural place—has been so embattled for its whole history that it's been forced to develop a distorted, contorted kind of a culture. What would the Jews of Europe, the refugees of Europe, have been able to do if they hadn't had that constant pressure around them at all times? If they hadn't been forced basically to live in a state of war for fifty years? I'm certainly not a cultural critic on Israel. I don't know that much about it. But I can't help thinking it would have been a very different place if the threat of constant warfare weren't there. So I think my book is a "What if?," but there is an "If only" wistfulness underlying the whole project.

Gaiman: Have you finished the book?

Chabon: I'm just starting. I'm off to a good start. Now people are giving me Yiddish books, Yiddish everything. I'm sure that happened when you were writing *American Gods*.

Gaiman: Are you getting the weird-coincidence world? I always find that, especially at the start of books.

Chabon: Yes. The coolest thing that happened so far has to do with how my narrator in this book refers to the United States. The book is set in the present day, so there's been a long, tortured relationship with the United States, which is sort of the sponsor of this country originally. The euphemism that is widely used by the people in this land for the United States is "Kindly Stepmother." I just wrote that—"our Kindly Stepmother to the south," and then I actually went to my Yiddish dictionary and looked up how you say *Kindly Stepmother* in Yiddish. *Kindly* is *frayndlekh* and *stepmother* is *shtif-mame*. "The United States" in Yiddish—I can't remember the word, but the initials are also "F.S." So it was like this perfect choice, but I didn't know it when I made it. I just made it.

Gaiman: I love the way those things happen.

Chabon: If they're not happening it's not a good sign.

Gaiman: The other one I always find is that the world starts offering you things. You'll be stuck on something and the next magazine you pick up will suggest an answer.

Chabon: Exactly. I love it when that happens. The example that I always think of is in *The Mysteries of Pittsburgh*, when I was writing the love scene between the two men, between Art and Arthur. I didn't know how to handle it. But I worked my way through it, and I finally felt like it was pretty good, but I didn't know how to end it. This is a scene where one character essentially loses his virginity. I was living in Newport Beach, and I walked down to the waterfront. A man was just coming toward me on the boardwalk. He had his head tilted back and a handkerchief pressed up against his nose. He had a bloody nose. I turned around and ran back and finished the scene. I realized that Art gets hit in the face in the course of his lovemaking, and his nose starts to bleed and the blood gets on the sheets, so then at the end of the scene Arthur takes the sheets and hangs them out the window the way they would do in primitive cultures.

Gaiman: To demonstrate that virginity had been taken.

Chabon: It was perfect. And it was all because I went for that walk and saw the guy with the bloody nose. There's a famous saying of Louis Pasteur's: "Chance favors the prepared mind." Or Branch Rickey, the great general manager of the Brooklyn Dodgers, had this saying: "Luck is the residue of design." When you're ready, when you've done your work, when you've prepared, when you know your subject backward and forward, those accidents happen. You just know what to do and what use to make of the things that fall to hand that way.

Escape Artistry

Pat Jankiewicz / 2004

From *STARLOG* January 2005: 54–59. © Fangoria Entertainment. Reprinted by permission.

Tall, long-haired and handsome, Michael Chabon looks more like a rock star than a writer. An author with a devoted following, he's the man responsible for such great books as *Summerland, Wonder Boys*, and *The Mysteries of Pittsburgh*. He has also won the Pulitzer Prize, which makes him the literary equivalent of a rock star.

Chabon earned the Pulitzer for *The Amazing Adventures of Kavalier & Clay*, an incredibly touching, epic novel about two friends who create a superhero at the dawn of the comic book industry. Chabon showed an uncanny knack for capturing the world of comics, their creators, and why comic book heroes resonate with the public at large.

He put those theories to the test when he helped create the story for director Sam Raimi's *Spider-Man 2*. In working to fashion a storyline that managed to balance the comic's humor and heroics with a nifty post-ironic spin, Chabon helped produce what is arguable the finest—and most faithful—comic book movie ever made.

"I grew up reading *STARLOG*. I just went through a big box of them that I had growing up," says Chabon, joined for this interview by his seven-year-old son, Zeke, who is wearing a "Roy the Toxic Boy" T-shirt.

Asked how he became involved with Your Friendly Neighborhood Spider-Man, Chabon professes, "It was very much out of the blue. I got a call from Sam Raimi, who told me, 'Spidey needs you!' I said, 'Of course, I would love to! Being asked to write for Peter Parker? How could I not?'

"They hired me to do a treatment outright, which they approved, and so I wrote a draft of the script. Then they said, 'Thank you, there's a lot of fine things in here. We're gonna take what you've done and give it to Alvin Sargent [the Oscar-winning screenwriter of *Paper Moon* and *Ordinary*

People].' They gave him [my script] and all the prior drafts they had at that point—including a David Koepp draft and one by Miles Millar and Alfred Gough. I don't know how Alvin proceeded, but what ended up on the screen had many elements drawn from Millar and Gough's draft and my script, but almost every word of dialogue was written by Alvin. I do have lines in the film, but not that many. Almost everything spoken was written by Alvin."

Amazing Fantasies

Chabon's main job was to make Aunt May's nephew totally miserable. "I was trying to be true to the spirit of the comics," he says. "The idea that Peter Parker just can't catch a break is a key element of the Spider-Man mythos, as developed from about issue #1 through the great epic of Gwen Stacy's death. The notion was, 'No matter what—even if things are getting better for him—something will happen'; whether it was Aunt May getting sick or marrying Doc Ock, something *always* went wrong. It wasn't my idea to put that in there; that came straight from Sam, who told me, 'I want you to make Peter the most miserable he has ever been. I want one thing after another after another. We have to pile it on.'

"I wrote a screenplay that was the third out of four drafts used. The humorous 'how hard it is to be Peter Parker' scenes I wrote tended to be the stuff they used in the final film. Less so, the fight scenes, action sequences, and supervillain ideas I came up with. They liked my 'human side of Peter Parker' material. I thought it would be funny to make him a pizza delivery boy. Even though that was rewritten, I enjoyed those scenes; they cracked me up."

Another Chabon addition was Peter's neighbor. "The Russian landlord was mine, and calling him 'Ditkovich' [after Spidey co-creator Steve Ditko] was also my idea," he says. "I was surprised that they kept what I thought was a silly joke. Alvin came up with Ditkovich's daughter [a shy girl who takes a liking to Peter]; I had nothing to do with her."

Chabon also tried to find a motive for the sequel's supervillain. "The idea was to humanize Doc Ock," he explains. "I tried to give Doc Ock a personality because, to be honest, Dr. Octopus in the comics had almost no personality. He's a cool concept and has those great arms, but Doc Ock is kind of a generic madman bent on destruction and mayhem. He has no real motivation. They've changed him over the years, from being sort of a spy to a career criminal to needing money or wanting revenge on Spider-Man.

"So because Doc Ock has no motives or personality, I thought this would be a good opportunity to give him some. The idea of trying to humanize him led to the idea that there's a parallel between Peter and Dr. Octopus. It was always there and obvious [in the comics], but never remarked on: Doc Ock is not really an octopus—he's a spider! He moves and crawls up walls like a spider; an octopus can't move like that. Clearly, there's a doubling layer there. Even their names, Otto Octavius and Peter Parker, both start with the same letters—although that was common for Stan Lee. It helped him remember the characters' names.

"Still, I saw that parallelism there—they both have these powers thrust on them by accident, and they both try to cope and contend with that. Ock fails and it gets the better of him—his legs, arms, pseudopods, whatever you want to call them, take over and control him. That *wasn't* in the comics. I tried to bring in a lot of stuff about the characters and the relationships between them.

"My favorite moment in the movie is also one that I wrote," he adds. "I took the famous collapsing wall from the Ditko art and had Peter go rescue Mary Jane. MJ says 'Hi' and Peter—who's holding up this wall to keep it from falling on her—says 'Hi . . . This is really heavy.'

"Alvin came up with Doc Ock's wife. Something I had that wouldn't have necessarily worked is that I had Doc Ock interested in Mary Jane. I made him a younger Doc Ock, and he makes a play for her," Chabon reveals. "She wasn't marrying John Jameson [in my story], so Ock was Peter's rival for her affections as well as the bad guy. They told me that they were thinking about getting a younger guy to play Doc Ock, so I immediately pictured Edward Norton. I don't know why, but imagining him as Doc Ock made it more interesting. I thought of ways to make him younger and sexier to MJ. It was fun to write him as young and hip. He worked as his own character, but I'm not sure he worked as Doc Ock. If they had kept me on, I probably would have changed that."

Marvel Tales

Swinging with Spidey "was fun—I really enjoyed inhabiting the world of Peter Parker," Chabon declares. "I've been a Spider-Man fan all of my life, so I went back and reread the entire continuity of *Amazing Spider-Man* from #1 to #120 [before writing the script]. I loved re-immersing myself into that incredible Ditko and John Romita artwork, and getting to write that and put words in the characters' mouths was a great experience. To be honest, [my involvement on *Spider-Man 2*] didn't last that long, and that was kind of a good thing, because I have many other projects that I'm working on. It could have been a long, drawn-out process, but it was short and sweet and they paid me very well, so I loved it!"

Rereading the classic web-spinner tales gave Chabon a better appreciation of Spidey co-creator Lee. "Stan's writing was incredibly lively," Chabon says. "It was self-mocking in a way that was very appealing, and the things Stan liked to write about appealed to the teenage imagination. His stories always said that it was hard to be different and that there's a lot of noble self-sacrifice by people who step up to the plate and do the right thing, even at the cost of their own lives—that was one of Stan's favorite subjects. That was very attractive to young readers. Also, the idea that people who seem evil often have a seed of goodness in them was another one of his favorite themes. It was great reading them all again."

Spider-Man 2 is a faithful adaptation of Lee and Romita's memorable *Amazing Spider-Man* #50, in which Peter renounces his crime-fighting crusade and dumps his costume in a trash can in a dark alley. "It's a great story and was a perfect choice for the movie," Chabon says. "It was Sam's idea. He asked me, 'Do you remember "Spider-Man No More?' I said, 'Yeah,' and he told me, 'That's what we want to do!'

"Sam is awesome," he declares. "Sam is just a great guy—sweet, thoughtful, attentive, and really intelligent. He's a decent person, and decent people aren't that common in the world, especially in Hollywood. That was the best part of all of it, working with Sam. What I liked about *Spider-Man* 2 had nothing to do with me or Alvin—even though it was well-written, especially for that kind of movie. What I loved about *Spider-Man* 2 is that it was so Sam Raimi.

"It was so much more a Sam Raimi movie than the first one: It looks like a Sam Raimi movie, and it feels like a Sam Raimi movie—especially with that horrific operating room scene. That was pure Raimi. I would put that up there with anything he did in *Army of Darkness*! As a fan of Sam Raimi films, I think *Spider-Man* 2 is one of his very best."

Before he got his Spider Sense, Tobey Maguire starred in another Chabon adaptation, *Wonder Boys*. "I thought he was great in *Wonder Boys*," Chabon extols. "[Director] Curtis Hanson made a really good film. I was cool with someone else scripting. That's how it is—if you don't want someone to mess with your book, don't sell it. No one forces authors to sell their books to Hollywood.

"Tobey is the perfect Peter Parker, and he's wonderful in the Spider-Man films. He's a great actor who accomplishes so much. He's a quiet, almost minimal performer who manages to convey an amazing range of emotions and feelings with a very soft voice and a face that isn't the most expressive in the world; yet somehow he uses that to indicate amazing tortured depth. That's more effective than a more expressive actor doing Jack Nicholson eyebrows and chewing the scenery."

Amazing Adventures

Chabon was born in Washington, DC, and mostly raised in that area. From "shortly after I was born until I was six years old, we moved all over the country because my Dad was in the service. Then we settled back in DC, where my parents are from. I grew up in Columbia, Maryland, a strange sort of planned city built in the '60s and '70s between Baltimore and Washington. That's where I first started reading *STARLOG*.

"I went to the University of Pittsburgh and lived there for a long time. I went to graduate school at UC Irvine, and since then I've lived in New York, Florida, Washington State, but mostly in California. Now, I live in Berkeley. I love Berkeley! I have the sandals for it," he jokes. "My wife Ayelet is also a writer. She has a series of mystery novels called *The Mommy-Track Mysteries*, about solving soccer-mom crimes. She has a new mystery novel out now."

Writing *Kavalier & Clay*, Chabon dealt with the amazing fantasies imagined and harsh realities endured by the first comics creators. "It was great to immerse myself in comic book history," he says. "Part of the reason I wanted to write it was so I would have an excuse to do that—just like an excuse to go back and reread all those *Spider-Man* comics. I decided to write *Kavalier & Clay* so I could revisit the old comics and read about them. I checked out magazines like *Comic Book Marketplace* and read interviews with the old creators. I also conducted interviews on my own, talking to guys like Stan, Gil Kane, and Will Eisner."

As comics sales have been declining for years, was Chabon surprised that *Kavalier & Clay* struck such a nerve with the more mainstream public? "Totally," he admits. "When I was writing it, I really did not know who would be interested in reading it, if anybody. I worried about that a lot!"

Researching the history of comics creators, Chabon was shocked to discover the sad lives many of the medium's founding fathers led. "Particularly [Superman creators] Jerry Siegel and Joe Shuster," he says. "Those guys had some really tough times. I was reading an article in *Smithsonian* magazine about Superman, and it mentioned how Siegel and Shuster dreamed up the character and sold it for $138. Even when I heard that as a kid, that chimed with me right away. My God, what a destiny: You create this fabulous character who goes on to conquer the world, and then what happened to them after that!

"*Smithsonian* didn't say much about what subsequently occurred," he continues, "but as I started researching it . . . The idea that Shuster was living on canned beans and going blind in that tiny apartment was so sad. It was almost too painful for me—I couldn't have that happen to the characters in my novel. That's why nothing like that is in *Kavalier*, because it's just too sad."

Kavalier and Clay are heading for Hollywood via producer Scott Rudin. "The screenplay is done," Chabon says. "I condensed, changed, and totally reconfigured some things. But it isn't drastically different from the book. It's essentially the same story with the same characters, but it's very different in the details. I had to do a lot of work!"

The fictional Kavalier and his comics co-creation were loosely based on real-life comics giant Jim Steranko and Jack Kirby's Mister Miracle (a character also based on Steranko). "Reading about Steranko's early career as an escape artist inspired me to give Joe Kavalier a similar career," Chabon says. "And the Escapist grew out of that. Mister Miracle had the same source of inspiration. So it's more accurate to say that they *both* derive from him."

Chabon's book also explores why many of the early comics creators were Jewish and the significance of their creations. "It's hard for me to sum up," he smiles. "That's why I wrote a whole novel!"

Winning the Pulitzer Prize for *Kavalier & Clay* "was one of the greatest days of my life," Chabon says. "It was so exciting, I still can't believe it. If I stop to think about it, it almost doesn't feel real—like they made a mistake. I *still* can't believe it."

The Escapist—the masked hero created by Chabon's Kavalier and Clay—now has his own comic book series, in which he continues to battle evil (with stories written by Chabon, Howard Chaykin, Mike Baron, Glen David Gold, and Kevin McCarthy, drawn by Gene Colan, Bill Sienkiewicz, Kyle Baker, Jim Starlin, and others). *The Escapist* marks the first time a Pulitzer Prize–winning novel has led to a superhero comic. "That's true," Chabon laughs. "It's cool. If Dark Horse Comics hadn't come to me with the idea, I probably would never have thought of that. It's not like I had said, 'Oooh, now that I created this great character, I'm going to do comic books about him.' But I'm *really* enjoying it."

Astonishing Tales

Growing up, Chabon's comic book tastes were eclectic. "I preferred the obscure stuff: *Omega the Unknown, Son of Satan, OMAC.* My favorite comic changed all the time. Mostly, I was loyal to the company—DC at first, and then Marvel when I got older. *Kamandi* had a major impact on me."

The author has formed a unique bond with his son through pop culture, as Zeke professes his undying love for Gigantor the Space-Age Robot. "I introduced him to *Gigantor*," Chabon says. "What's cool is that many of the things I remember loving as a kid are either still there—like Superman, Batman, and Spider-Man—or they've been revived. *Gigantor* has been gone awhile, although he's out there again. I remember watching *Astro Boy* when I was six years old, and then he disappeared completely from my life. But now he's *really* back," Chabon remarks, referring to the *Astro Boy* animated feature being directed by Genndy (*Samurai Jack*) Tartakovsky.

"There's all this stuff that we can share, and it *isn't* an exercise in nostalgia, the way it was for me as a kid," he muses. "I was into hearing what my father remembered from his childhood; I loved learning about radio programs he listened to, the pop culture, the Big Little Books, and the comic books, of course. My dad told me about the Marx Brothers as a kid, but there was only one Marx Brothers book in my library, a fotonovela. That was my only access to the Marx Brothers because there were no VCRs.

"My father's childhood pop culture was this lost kingdom, and many years went by before I could even access that stuff and be able to see it, touch it, and own it. For Zeke, there isn't any gap; it's continual. He can see *Speed Racer, Gigantor,* and *Kimba the White Lion.* He especially likes Japanese robots, so when a Gigantor toy caught Zeke's eye at a con, he asked me, 'What's that?' I said, 'Oh, that's Gigantor.'"

Zeke adds that he and his father "like the *Gundam*s, *Ultraman,* and *8 Man.*" Chabon notes, "Zeke recognizes *Johnny Sokko and His Flying Robot,* but he has never seen it; I've just told him about it. We got the original *Ultraman* [show] at a con. We decided that what was good about *Ultraman* is that the monster always appears in the first five minutes."

"We like it when the monster shows up fast!" Zeke pipes in. "We saw *The Hulk* and the Hulk didn't show up for 300 hours!"

"That can be frustrating for us," Chabon laughs. "Zeke watched a *Mechagodzilla* movie the other day, and an hour in, no monsters had shown up yet! We had all the 'O no, the meters are reading 300, Professor!' scenes, but not Godzilla. With *Ultraman*, the monster is always knocking things over in the first five minutes!"

Journeys into Mystery

Watching stuff he loved as a kid through his son's eyes "gives me a totally new perspective," Chabon grins. "It's really fun. I even let him look at my comics from the '70s. They're in my office. I have a spinner rack that says 'COMIC BOOKS ARE FUN!' with Richie Rich, Spider-Man, Superman, and Archie on it. It's full of comics that can get messed up; there's nothing valuable on the rack. I have a drawer where I keep the important ones.

"Both Zeke and Sophie, his older sister, are into comics," says Chabon, who also has two younger children, Ida-Rose and Abraham. "Sophie just read *From the Ashes* and *X-Men: The Dark Phoenix Saga*. She likes the X-Men and strong female characters. Chris Claremont [who penned *The Dark Phoenix Saga*] is known for writing strong women. I've always liked Chris, but that was one aspect of his work I never paid any attention to. Now that I have a daughter, I really appreciate the quality and centrality of female characters in his work, like Jean Grey and Storm. When I started writing *Summerland*, I knew that I had to put a strong female character in there, or else Sophie wouldn't like it.

"It's like a handcrafted approach to creating a comic book fan. But it's hard to find [suitable] comics for my children. I get them reprints of the ones I remember, because most of the stuff being put out now is inappropriate or uninteresting for kids. Comics can't just be about toys and action figures; they have to be something kids can *read*, too. I'm relying on twenty-year-old *X-Men* reprints and, in Zeke's case, forty-year-old *Legion of Super-Heroes*.

"Some of the stuff out there is good for kids, like *Bone*," Chabon observes. "But I don't see much storytelling in today's comics, just a lot of set-ups for battles. The *Legion of Super-Heroes* stories from the late '50s and early '60s were written by great comics writers. Jerry Siegel and Edmond Hamilton did many of them, and they were great. They had plots, mysteries, puzzles, and stories that weren't just excuses for the big battle at the end. Sometimes, there wasn't any battle at all. I believe storytelling is the key to comics' future for kids."

Reading to his kids at night helped inspire Chabon to write his fantasy novel *Summerland*. "I rediscovered books that I loved as a kid and thought about writing [a children's fantasy]." *Summerland* has a diverse supporting cast of fantasy characters, including the elusive half-man/half-ape known as Sasquatch. "The story is woven out of American folklore and fairy tales. Sasquatch is a key piece of American folklore for me, and *Summerland* takes place in an American mythological universe."

Chabon was in the running to write the first *X-Men* movie. "I did a treatment and tried to get myself the scripting job," he confirms. "I was trying to persuade them to hire me, and I almost had them, when Bryan Singer showed up. He already had a writer he worked with, so they made the correct, obvious choice. There was lots of action in my pitch.

"My main point [in my *X-Men* pitch] was that I didn't want to use *any* supervillains—there was no Magneto or Brotherhood of Evil mutants. I think there are too many people in costumes in *X-Men*, and I wanted the audience to get their minds around the concept of the X-Men. I liked both of Singer's X-Men films; I liked their seriousness. The comic has always been very somber with elements of humor. It has a weighty feel to it, and the movies capture that."

Next up for Chabon is scripting *Snow and the Seven*. It retells the fairy tale, substituting seven Shaolin monks and martial arts. *Matrix* action maestro Yuen Woo-ping will direct for Disney.

Asked if he has ever considered writing the comic book adventures of Spider-Man or the Escapist on a monthly basis, Chabon replies, "Nah, I don't think I could spare that amount of time. I've had several offers to write various titles over the past few years, and *Spider-Man* may have been one of them. DC asked if I wanted to do something original or take over a book, but that's hard. Writing comics is so much work—for me, anyway. I'm slow and it takes me a long time, so I don't think it would be cost-effective and, as you know, it doesn't pay very well. I don't think I could manage it."

But how would he respond, should his phone ring one dark and stormy night, and Sam Raimi said, "Mike, Spidey needs you again"? "Oh, absolutely," Michael Chabon grins. "I would do it in a heartbeat!"

Michael Chabon:
Pulp, Comics, and Baseball

Locus / 2004

From *Locus: The Magazine of the Science Fiction and Fantasy Field* December 2004: 6, 71–72.
© *Locus*. Reprinted by permission.

Michael Chabon was born May 24, 1963 in Washington, DC, and raised in a utopian community in Columbia, Maryland. He attended the University of Pittsburgh, receiving a BA in 1984 in English literature, then an MFA at the University of California at Irvine; his master's thesis became his first novel, bestselling coming-of-age story *The Mysteries of Pittsburgh* (1988). His other novels are *Wonder Boys* (1995), Pulitzer Prize winner *The Amazing Adventures of Kavalier & Clay* (2000), and Mythopoeic Award–winning YA *Summerland* (2002), with historical mystery *The Final Solution* and alternate history *The Yiddish Policemen's Union* forthcoming. He has published two collections, *A Model World and Other Stories* (1991) and *Werewolves in Their Youth* (1999), and edited print anthology *McSweeney's Enchanted Chamber of Astonishing Stories* (2004) and comic book anthologies *The Amazing Adventures of the Escapist* Volumes 1 and 2, based on his character from *The Amazing Adventures of Kavalier & Clay*.

Chabon lives with his wife, writer Ayelet Waldman (married 1993), in Berkeley, California. They have four children.

"It's quite obvious to me that so much of what goes on in the world of science fiction has analogies with a ghetto mentality, with a sense of clannishness and that ambivalence that you have: on the one hand wanting to keep outsiders *out* and identify all the insiders with a special language and jargon so you can tell at a glance who does and doesn't belong, and on the other hand hating that sense of confinement, wanting to move beyond the walls of the ghetto and find wider acceptance. It's a deep ambivalence. You want both at the same time: you feel confined, and you feel supported and protected. I've talked about this with Jonathan Lethem, who says we seem to be moving in opposite directions; he's moving out of the genre and working his way toward a wider mainstream readership, while I wrote a fantasy novel and now I'm doing alternate history.

"I'm not alone in the kinds of things I do—and sometimes that bothers me! I was very dismayed when I was about halfway through *Summerland* and this book *American Gods* by Neil Gaiman came in the mail, with *his* version of this country's mythology. I put it aside. The same thing happened previously when I was writing *Kavalier & Clay* and was sent Tom De Haven's *Derby Dugan's Depression Funnies*. The idea was so similar to mine, I just had to banish it from the house! Now I'm working on a novel set in an alternate-historical timeline where there's no Israel, and in World War II the United States allowed a lot of Jewish refugees into the Alaskan Territories to settle, so they started this Yiddish-speaking territory. And Philip Roth decides he has to write a novel with an alternate-history Jewish World War II timeline!

"My novel is called *The Yiddish Policemen's Union*. I can't speak Yiddish much; I just very slowly and painstakingly read it now, with a dictionary. My great-grandparents and my great-aunt used it, and they only used it when they didn't want us to know what they were saying. My wife's Jewish too, and it's definitely part of the language of our house. As soon as we had our first child, Yiddish words about babies and children started coming out of our mouths. And all the terms of disparagement for other people, and so on—that's part of our active vocabulary.

"In my initial ideas of wanting to edit my own magazine, the project that became *McSweeney's*, pulps were only part of what I was thinking of (although you wouldn't know that from the packaging!). With my own short stories I felt confined, and out of that sense of confinement and disappointment with them, I started going back, looking at short stories that meant something to me. The farther I went back, to things like Bradbury's 'The Rocket Man' and Edgar Allan Poe's stories and the first short stories I had ever read, I started to notice they were genre, whether science fiction or mystery or horror. Then I started looking at these old authors and collections. The ones between 1850 and 1950, whether they're considered today 'literary' writers or precursors of genre fiction, were writing genre fiction: ghost stories, horror stories, sea stories, and westerns.

"That made me wonder, what happened to all those? We still have genre short story writers, but what happened to the whole thing? Why aren't people who *aren't* considered genre writers—people writing what they consider to be mainstream or literary fiction—writing ghost stories and more? Henry James wrote ghost stories. So did Edith Wharton. Robert Graves wrote an incredibly wonderful ghost story called 'The Shout.' It wasn't considered slumming or betraying your art; it was just considered part of your ordinary tool kit as a writer. So I thought, 'Maybe I should try that.' And then, 'Maybe we should *all* try it and see what happens.' The more I thought about it, the more the whole idea of there being distinctions between genres, and between genre writers and literary writers (particularly *that* distinction), just seemed arbitrary, capricious, and hard to justify.

"It's not only confining to genre writers—*I* felt confined by that barrier too. So much of what I grew up reading and loving, and books I continue to read, were originally labeled as genre. Raymond Chandler, one of my favorite writers, has finally been elevated into the pantheon of literary writers. There's a few like that, who came out of the pulps. There was once a world of short stories in magazines, written by writers with artistic ambition and intention but also popular and successful, and *part* of that was the pulps. It was also happening in the *New Yorker* and *Collier's* and *Saturday Evening Post*, a lot of the outlets. (F. Scott Fitzgerald wrote 'The Diamond as Big as the Ritz,' an adventure story.)

"I always am attracted to situations where the barriers aren't very strong. I decided I didn't like feeling like I was on a reservation—like a lot of writers, who are on *various* reservations—and I wanted to try to create a space in which both writers who are viewed primarily as genre writers and writers viewed primarily as *not* genre writers could come together. Literary ones could write stories with more plot (that was going to be a side benefit), but would have the liberty to write a story that *wasn't* a slice-of-life, epiphany-based thing—what they call 'the *New Yorker* story,' although I don't think that's really a fair description. (A lot of John Cheever's early works in the *New Yorker* weren't chronicles of suburban angst, but kind of horror or supernatural stories.)

"In the second *McSweeney's*, for some reason, the preponderance of stories are what I'd call supernatural horror, ghost stories in the kind of creepy vein. I couldn't finish one this time, since I'm stuck in a new novel and couldn't take the time away from the book to do it, but my wife has a really creepy story in it. Other contributors include Peter Straub, China Miéville, Poppy Z. Brite, Joyce Carol Oates, and Stephen King (he's the only person who's back from the first one). In my introduction I talk about the whole packaging thing, how the same book can be presented differently for genre or mainstream audiences. First of all, it's apparent that by virtue of changing the artwork and typeface on the jacket, and the overall look of a book, you can completely alter the way someone's going to interpret it. (That also applies if you change the font inside the book; if you use a more distinguished-looking font like a Garamond.) It doesn't always work, but it has for reprints of people like Philip K. Dick and Raymond Chandler. If the writing is there, the ideas are there, the quality and the content is there, it will work. Niffenegger's *The Time Traveler's Wife* was a huge bestseller, but if they had published that book as a science fiction novel, people would just avoid it by virtue of the fact that it was so labeled.

"You *do* judge a book by its cover—or which section of the bookstore you bought it in. What if they made a bookstore that just had a fiction section, and *all* fiction was in it? I want to own a bookstore like that someday.

"I have a big collection of old science fiction and fantasy. Some of these books I had never even heard of when I picked them up. If I consider the *writing* good, I can read almost anything, no matter how old it is. Things like Poul Anderson's *The Broken Sword*. Fritz Leiber was a really good writer, and Ray Bradbury. Bradbury's short stories were key for me. Those were some of the first stories I ever read thinking, 'These are great works of art,' when I was thirteen or fourteen years old. When I read them now, part of my response is that deep, layered, buried old response—I remember how I felt when I was reading them for the first time—but they're still good. Clifford D. Simak is another; it's still spellbinding. Sturgeon was one of my key writers too. I just loved *More Than Human*. I reread it about five years ago, and it's still a powerful book. Jack Vance's writing, his style, was another very strong influence. And works by Richard Lupoff, like a story I read when I was around fourteen, where the writing's really sparkly and flashy and show-offy—I was really into that. And his *All in Color for a Dime* was a book I used heavily when I was writing *Kavalier & Clay*.

"I did a lot of research and reading before I wrote that book, and I conducted interviews, but the genesis of it, the germ of it and whatever verisimilitude it as, comes from growing up hearing my father talking about his youth. I don't know what I'm thinking at all, until I've written it—then I find out!—and *Kavalier & Clay* was an unending series of surprises. I started it with the sketchiest idea of wanting to write a novel set during the golden age of comic books, and maybe there'd be two guys. . . . I had no idea I was going to be writing about Prague, no idea the golem was going to play a role, that there was going to be a section set in the Antarctic, or anything about magic and Houdini's escape artistry. All that stuff didn't come out of the story I was telling but out of my just stumbling on connections among things I had not noticed before. For instance I had never noticed that the golem, at least as he was initially conceived, was a kind of precursor of the superhero idea: a super-being who defends the meek and the oppressed. A lot of readers are puzzled by the return of the golem late in the book. There's the Chekhov 'gun on the wall' aspect to it, but also I couldn't send Joe Kavalier back to Europe after the war, in terms of the kind of story I was trying to tell. So I had to have someone in Europe come to him, so we could 'see' the devastation without seeing the devastation.

"*Summerland* grew directly out of my childhood reading. In fact, the initial idea for it came to me when I was a child. I was reading a lot of fantasy based on Celtic, Scandinavian, and British mythology—C. S. Lewis, Tolkien, Susan Cooper, Lloyd Alexander. I loved them, but I was also into American folklore and tall tales, and Native American legends. I remember thinking, 'I wonder if you could write a novel that would be like these books but would draw on *American* mythology and folklore.' I took the idea and put it away. It really wasn't until I had kids of my own and was reading to them those very books *I'd* read—that started me thinking again, and remembering that my original ambition as a writer was to write the kind of book that became *Summerland*.

"Another important element of *Summerland* is baseball. There must be something about baseball! Without trying to make too much out of the symbolism—'home' and 'the base paths' and all that—it's a sport where you have (as you do in so many epic adventures) this battle at the heart of it, between the pitcher and the batter. Even though they belong to a sort of army as a member of a team, when you get right down to it it's one-to-one, man-to-man battle. So you have this strange dynamic between the team and the individual. There's no other sport remotely like that. Baseball is quirky and crotchety and peculiar, with things that don't make sense at the level that most other sports make sense, and that makes it fertile ground for imagination to take over. It's also caught up in American history and Americans' idea of themselves as no other sport has been. So you have Walt Whitman writing about baseball. During the Civil War, the guys from New York and Boston were playing the game in their downtime, and they taught it to their fellow soldiers from all over the country, including the South. It spread from there.

"At this year's Comic-Con, I gave the Eisner speech, talking about my idea that children didn't abandon comics; comics abandoned children. They did it very calculatedly and avowedly: 'Let's start making comics for older readers.' It started in some ways with EC Comics in the early '50s, then Marvel in the '60s, but really took off with the rise of the independents in the 1980s. I'm not saying it's a bad thing, not criticizing that at all. It's a completely laudable ambition, and I'm very grateful for all this great work that's been done for an adult readership. Again, there's a certain amount of parallel with the ghetto mentality and the ghetto desire to assimilate. Part of that is, you try to cover up your roots when you start making it. Comics did that. They tried—with complete justification, because of the brutal treatment their art has received for so long—to distance themselves from the idea that they were 'greasy kids' stuff.' All I was trying to point out was that *now*, when comics have achieved at least a measure of critical respect (they're being reviewed in the *New York Times Book Review* and the *New York Review of Books*, for godsake!), it's time to relax a little bit.

"Furthermore, there's this undeniable dwindling of comic book readership that's been taking place since the mid-'50s, and then drastically in the past ten to fifteen years: the audience has shrunk and shrunk. So now you've got a lot of really great comic books being made for older readers, but that's all you've got. With my son and daughter, I've *forced* them to like comics. I kept at them: 'Isn't this good?' and 'Don't you like this?' Finally, now my daughter is ten, I got her to read some Chris Claremont *X-Men* comics. She loved them and wanted more—it had finally worked! I felt like I was fanning this tiny flame and trying to keep it from the wind. And the wind is the wind of indifference, coming both from the comic book industry and from the culture around her, and the children around her who don't read comics or talk about comics. But we can't all afford to take that handcrafted approach, promoting it one kid at a time.

"People say, 'Oh, there's too much competition with videogames and movies and computers and the Internet,' blah blah blah. I think it's a naïve perspective, as if all there was to do when you were a kid in 1938 was sit around and read comic books. No way! There were two million other things you could be doing in 1938 when Superman first came out—there was a whole street life, all this free entertainment out there! Comic books didn't succeed then because they were the only game in town; they succeeded because they were aimed, marketed, sold, and distributed with children in mind. They were priced right, and they were ubiquitous: on every corner newsstand, in the drug store, in the candy store. . . . Now they're only in comic book stores, and an eight-year-old nowadays isn't going to wander into a comic book store."

Arctic Jews:
An Interview with Michael Chabon

Jon Wiener / 2007

From *Dissent* 14 April 2007. Web. Reprinted by permission.

Like Philip Roth's *The Plot against America*, Michael Chabon's newest novel, *The Yiddish Policemen's Union*, is set in a counterfactual world. In Chabon's retelling of history, the US permitted European Jews fleeing Hitler to settle in Sitka, a small fishing town in Alaska. After the 1948 defeat of the nascent state of Israel, the city becomes the improbable center of a new Jewish homeland—one where the language remains primarily Yiddish. The book is, among other things, a gripping murder mystery set in the "present" as the settlement is preparing to revert back to Alaskan control. Chabon won the 2001 Pulitzer Prize for his novel, *The Amazing Adventures of Kavalier & Clay*. *Dissent* contributor Jon Wiener ("The Weatherman Temptation," Spring 2007) caught up with him in Los Angeles.

Jon Wiener: You say it's a fact that FDR suggested Alaska as a temporary homeland for the displaced Jews of Second World War Europe. I never heard that before.

Michael Chabon: It wasn't FDR himself, it was Harold Ickes, his Secretary of the Interior. The proposal was couched in terms of exploiting the Alaskan territory and its resources, the huge untapped wealth up there. We need people up there. Nobody really wants to go up there. Where could we find some people who would want to go up there? I know: there are these millions of people in Europe now who are clamoring to get out, desperate to get out; why don't we kill two birds with one stone and let them go there? But we won't let them go anywhere else, and they won't be granted any kind of permanent residency status. When the war is over, they can go back.

JW: How far did this Harold Ickes proposal get?

MC: It got to Congress. A bill was introduced in the Committee on Insular Affairs, I think it was, where it died. There was very strong opposition from the establishment in Alaska. Alaskan lumber and mining and other interests were dead set against having this unwashed immigrant population come in and sully this pristine wilderness.

JW: I get the picture.

MC: So the man who was the nonvoting delegate of the territory of Alaska, but who nevertheless had some influence, spearheaded the opposition in committee. The bill was quickly defeated and never made it onto the floor.

JW: However in the book—

MC: Yes, in the novel, this delegate was dining at Hogate's seafood restaurant in Washington, DC, an establishment once famous for its rum buns. I remember eating them myself as a kid, and they were quite delicious. He drops one of his rum buns when he's coming out of the restaurant. In his haste to get it, he chases it into the street, where he's run over by a passing taxicab and killed. In my story this bill is passed and becomes law and the Jews are admitted. They come in several waves, first in 1940, and then after the war more come, and then many more in 1948 after the collapse of the state of Israel. Israel collapses partly because the United States, having done this grand gesture, doesn't feel the same sense of guilt and the same pressure to do something to help the Zionists in Israel. Therefore the fledgling state of Israel is overwhelmed and defeated, and after that a lot more refugees come to Alaska.

JW: This is a book about the world of Yiddish—the language of the Yids. How come you know so much about Yiddish?

MC: The truth is I don't actually know any Yiddish really. I can't speak two sentences of Yiddish. I can read it with a lot of trouble. I can vaguely understand things said to me. I did a lot of research and tried to teach myself on my own, as much as I needed to write this book.

JW: This is something you've been interested in for a long time, going back to *Kavalier & Clay* days.

MC: It is. I wrote an essay published about ten years ago that was a response to this phrase book that you can buy in a bookstore called *Say It in Yiddish:*

A Phrase Book for Travelers. It's not a joke, it's divided into the usual sections: how to deal with government bureaucrats in Yiddish, how to make your way through an airport in Yiddish—

JW: What airport is this?
MC: Precisely. That was the point of the essay: to try to speculate on where you could go with this book. Realizing there was no actual place where you would need this book, I tried to dream up some imaginary destinations where such a book might come in handy. And I dwelled a little bit on this Alaska thing in that essay, just for a paragraph. But I found I couldn't get it out of my head.

I always wanted to know more about Yiddish. I grew up hearing it all the time, spoken by the grandparents' generation. I had a great-great aunt who was a regular reader of *The Forward* in Yiddish. I was very aware of Yiddish, but I did not understand it, so that immersion and alienation from the language had a strong impact on me. And I found when I started to write this novel that I could hear the sound of Yiddish, and it influenced the style in English of this book.

JW: *The Yiddish Policemen's Union* is in part a mystery story—our protagonist is a Jewish homicide detective.
MC: Yes. Whatever else this book may or may not be, it is also a murder mystery. I wanted to write a detective story that a reader of detective stories would read and love.

JW: The book suggests that you have some affection for a genre from an earlier era, stories about a down-at-the-heels dick on a caper.
MC: Yes. Raymond Chandler is one of my favorite writers. I go back and reread his books pretty regularly, particularly *The Long Goodbye*. I think it's one of the great American novels. And I also love and admire Ross Macdonald, whose novels I think surpass Chandler's on a technical level, in their construction. They're not quite as much fun as Chandler, and that might explain why he's unjustly forgotten now. His novels are still in print, and people still read them, but I wish he were better known.

Both Chandler's hero, Philip Marlowe, and Ross Macdonald's Lew Archer are in the same mold: solitary, isolated men. They don't have girlfriends, they live alone in apartments, drinking themselves to sleep at night over their books of chess problems. I wanted to play with that, in the most fond and affectionate sense. I'm not trying to write parody or pastiche, I'm really trying to engage with the work of these writers I love so much and whose novels mean so much to me.

JW: Part of this genre is a deep immersion in a place. For these two writers, it's Los Angeles. But you have done something they didn't do: you have imaged a whole new place. Sitka, Alaska, the site of your story, is in reality just a dumpy little town that fills up with cruise ship passengers several times a week during the summer.

MC: That's a really good point, and in that respect the framework of the detective novel served me well. It wasn't the most conscious decision that I've ever made, but I made an intuitive decision that if I was going to describe the world of this Yiddish-speaking district in Alaska, I was going to need a narrative framework that enabled me to have access to every aspect and layer of that world. I wanted to present it in *toto* to the reader. A lot of other possibilities could have occurred to me: an omniscient narrator, a Dickensian narrator, probably would have worked also. But right away I thought of this detective figure who is able to go anywhere, see anything, talk to anyone. This is not a private detective, this is a homicide detective, so his badge gets him in any door. No doors are closed to him. Not only that, he also understands the inner workings of his society. He knows which wheels are getting the most grease. It seemed like the right choice for a figure to be a guide for the reader into this Jewish inferno.

JW: This is also a story about a superman with a hidden identity, a kind of Clark Kent of the Jews. But your Clark Kent doesn't want to be the Jewish Superman.

MC: That's very true. He's a superman who has refused the cape. This man was a prodigy. Many great expectations were raised about him when he was a child. He was a chess prodigy and also a prophesied chosen one of his people. A man of great abilities, great sensitivity, great tenderness, great ability to connect with others—a Jewish Bill Clinton in many ways.

JW: And yet he's a heroin addict.

MC: He couldn't handle it. He couldn't take the overwhelming responsibly of being able to connect so powerfully with people. So he's living very much alone, as a heroin addict, in this cheap hotel in which our hero, Detective Meyer Landsman, also lives, and in which he meets his death at the very opening of the novel.

JW: The Third Temple in Jerusalem figures in your story. The first two of course were destroyed in ancient times. I remember walking around Jerusalem in the Jewish Quarter of the old city and coming across an upscale place that was displaying a model of the Third Temple, to be built according to architectural instructions in the Bible. Black-hatted Jews with beards stood outside urging me and everybody else, "Come in, take a look!" I was horrified because I knew where they want to build this temple.

MC: I've been there too. It's not just that model they have on display. They also have all the implements on display as well. In certain reviews of this book the sentiment has been expressed that, if anything is marring this book, it's this farfetched element of these fanatical people who want to see the Third Temple constructed in Jerusalem. Unfortunately, as you mentioned, where there once was a temple there is now this incredibly important Muslim shrine that was built in seventh century.

JW: We call it the Dome of the Rock.

MC: And if a temple ever were to be built on that site, somebody would have to do something about that mosque. These people with their institute in Jerusalem with their model and their implements—they don't really like to talk about how the space for the temple is going to be cleared. They don't want to go into that. It's often said that has been left in the hands of God, which terrifies me. This is not farfetched. It's very much a real thing. There are people out there who are evangelical cattle breeders, you can see pictures on the internet of the various attempts, thus far unsuccessful, to breed a red heifer, which is necessary for the fulfillment of certain prophecies associated with the rebuilding of the temple and the coming of the messiah. That's one of the things I didn't have to make up for this novel.

JW: I've heard that the Jews can be argumentative. Has anybody been outraged by the portrayal of Jews in your book? Have you been called a self-hating Jew?

MC: So far the only person who has said such a thing was not himself Jewish, so his credentials, in my view, seemed a little bit impeachable. But it's traditional for American Jewish writers that, if you depict Jewish characters engaged in some of the less admirable kinds of behavior that human beings engage in all over the planet, like greed, rapacity, violence, intolerance, if you attribute such behavior to Jews, some Jews get upset about that. They accuse you, in the Yiddish formulation, of "making a *shande* for the *goyim*": airing dirty laundry in public, making a display of disunity at a time when unity is so important. It doesn't matter what time it is, it's always a time when unity is so important. The great example was pointed out to me by my mother, in the aftermath of some criticism of my work: Philip Roth, who many times in his career has been accused of this, for many books, starting at the very beginning with *Goodbye, Columbus*. My mom said it was proof that I had finally arrived.

"Metaphor for the Imagination": A Conversation with Michael Chabon

Susan Breitkopf / 2007

From *Museum* January/February 2008: 48–52. © American Alliance of Museums. Reprinted with permission.

Costumed, comic book adventure heroes in New York, a drunken rogue cop in a Jewish homeland in Alaska, inebriated Vikings and rampaging elephants in a Byzantine-era kingdom. Michael Chabon's fictional landscapes are considerably more fictional and a lot wilder than those you will find in Hemingway, Edith Wharton, Philip Roth, or any number of other celebrated novelists working in the American realist tradition. Winner of the 2001 Pulitzer Prize for fiction, Chabon defies an easy categorization. He draws from and mixes popular and pulp sources, obscure corners of world history and his own Jewish roots in crafting his often comic and always engrossing literature.

His first novel, *The Mysteries of Pittsburgh* (1988), was published when he was just twenty-four. In 2000, Chabon published *The Amazing Adventures of Kavalier & Clay*, a novel that won him the Pulitzer. Other novels include *Wonder Boys*, the young adult novel *Summerland*, *The Yiddish Policemen's Union*, and, most recently, *Gentlemen of the Road*, serialized in the *New York Times*. He has also authored two collections of short stories, *A Model World and Other Stories* and *Werewolves in Their Youth*.

Museum Managing Editor Susan Breitkopf recently spoke with Chabon about his early experiences in museums, why you can't go home again, and where he's going next.

Museum: It seems that your writing has a lot in common with what many museums do: there is an effort to interpret and analyze the past or even wildly re-create it. How have museums influenced you?

Michael Chabon: I don't have any doubt that museums or my experience of museum-going—starting when I was a child—played a really powerful role in shaping my imagination and my sense of the past, certainly. And, you know, I grew up outside of Washington, DC, and was a very frequent visitor to the Smithsonian and others, like the Ford's Theatre museum. My entire sense of my history as an American was so overwhelmingly shaped by what I saw and heard in the museums in Washington. The whole city felt kind of like a combination of shrine and museum to a version of the American past. And when I was growing up in the late '60s, early '70s, there wasn't a whole lot of revisionism going on then. It was more the old-fashioned physical history. It was very powerful narrative, and I think one that I feel very much engaged with in my work and my writing, especially when I was writing *The Amazing Adventures of Kavalier & Clay*. I think that is part of the relationship.

I also always respond to the image in both my imagination and my relatively more limited experience of the basements and storage areas of museums and the idea of a museum itself. It's a sort of rummage sale or curiosity shop. There's a kind of chaotic accumulation of symmetry that is buried beneath the museum or in its attic.

I had this very important experience in my life. At one time, when I was a kid, I was lost in the basement of the Carnegie Institute in Pittsburgh with my brother. We were looking for a way out, and we kept going the wrong way; it's become somewhat mythologized in my mind. But I remember looking into these rooms that we weren't supposed to look into and seeing vast collections of what appeared to be discarded exhibits and/or things that were no longer being used. And I was feeling like I was at the bottom of the city of Pittsburgh looking at all of this stuff. It was really a powerful moment for me.

I don't know exactly how this all ties together, but I guess it's like there's a metaphor for the imagination, a metaphor for the storytelling imagination in museums.

Museum: Museum people would be thrilled to hear that kind of interpretation. That's what they're shooting for. So do you do any research at museums now?

MC: When I was working on *The Amazing Adventures of Kavalier & Clay*, I went to New York for a month and made a number of museum visits to the New York Historical Society, the Tenement Museum, a lot of the museums on the history of New York City, as well as going back to the Metropolitan Museum of Art several times just because it was part of the whole world of New York that I was trying to immerse myself in.

Museum: Is your family originally from New York?

MC: Well, parts of them; parts of my family came through New York—originally they're from Russia and Poland and Lithuania. And several branches ended up in New York before moving elsewhere, whereas others came through Philadelphia or other ports of entry.

Museum: It just seems that in *Kavalier & Clay* you built your characters and storylines on some sort of family experience.

MC: Absolutely. My dad grew up in Brooklyn in the '30s, '40s, '50s, so my main portal to the path in New York City was through my dad and his stories, his memories of growing up there.

Museum: From what I read, the different types of popular cultures in your book, whether it's Yiddish popular culture or other types, have made critics kind of crazy in terms of trying to fit your work into a genre. Where did those influences come from?

MC: Well, I think anybody who's my age [forty-four] or younger had no choice in the matter. We grew up in a world in which television was already very firmly established. I grew up in the '60s when the whole pop art movement was working very hard to break down or erase the last of the remaining barriers between high art and low art.

I think it's much more a reflection of the overall climate and culture of the time that I grew up in. And as I got older, I found myself living in a world in which mixing and matching, sampling, blending of genres was increasingly the norm in a lot of the art that I was being exposed to—whether in popular music or classical music or visual arts. It feels very inevitable. It's not a deliberate program or an agenda so much as just a natural approach.

Museum: What other kinds of things have influenced your work?

MC: I'm a huge movie fan. And my overall interest in the past and in history definitely forms part of my understanding of [current] movies and old movies. My favorite movies, once again, were the ones I watched with my dad—the experience of watching movies from his childhood, starting with a movie he remembered growing up with, silent films, to the movies he watched as a kid. That's part of my standard diet.

Museum: What are your favorite museums? Which ones do you take your kids to?

MC: Well, whenever we're in New York, we always have to go to the American Museum of Natural History. I guess the museum we've been to the most in the immediate past has been the Asian Art Museum in San Francisco because they've had a few shows there that we've all taken an interest in. They did this great show of Tezuka Osamu, the creator of a lot of Japanese comics, including *Astro Boy*. They did a fantastic show of lots of his original artwork and looked at his importance in Japanese popular culture. It was an exhibition that was well aimed at both kids and adults.

Museum: Given the experience you had going to museums growing up, are you trying to give your kids the same sort of thing?

MC: No knock on the museums that we have in San Francisco or the Bay Area, but growing up down the street from the Smithsonian, I took it for granted as a kid. I did not at all understand what an immense, almost in some ways overpowering kind of museum experience the Smithsonian was. I just sort of thought that was my neighborhood museum because we made so many trips both for school field trips and with my family. I can remember the incredible excitement I felt when the National Air and Space Museum opened. I was there opening week. At the time I was a huge space and science fiction aficionado, and I felt like that was my museum; it had been built for me and satisfied all my interests and desires. There's not going to be any way to really replicate that.

When I was in high school, I started to get really interested in art and painting, especially modern paintings. And when the Hirshhorn opened, I can remember that very well, going there in its first weeks. And then the I. M. Pei galleries—that wing they added to the National Gallery—that was a really exciting moment for me because I was just at my peak of interest in twentieth-century art and architecture. There was this sense as I was growing up that no matter what I was interested in, no matter at what level I wanted to approach art and culture through a museum, there was one there waiting for me already. And it wasn't just any museum. It was a really great museum. I don't quite feel like I can offer my kids the same.

Museum: So when you've visited Washington more recently, have you felt the same kind of magic that you did when you were a kid?

MC: The couple of times we've gone to DC with some or all of our children, we have taken them to various museums. And you have those powerful moments of reconnecting. There are certain bits and pieces that look the same or look as I remember them when walking into what was the Museum of Natural History or Air and Space Museum. Standing at that incredibly narrow, pointy corner of the East Wing of the National Gallery, where everyone goes and puts their hands on that jutting big old stone—I have these moments of reconnection. But when you're experiencing something with your children, that only lasts a little while. And then pretty quickly your new experience that they're going through with you supplants what you remember.

Museum: And you can't go home again, I guess.

MC: Exactly. And they've all been changed so much. The last time I was in DC and I went to the United States Holocaust Memorial Museum, which I had not been to before—it wasn't there when I was growing up.

Museum: What was that experience like? How did that inform you?

MC: Well, it was pretty devastating. It's beautiful, but it's horrible. Though it was fantastically well designed. It was a powerful way to spend the hours. I didn't gain any real additional knowledge or information. It was more of a gaining of experience. I think the thing that struck me most powerfully in there was that sense of how deeply rooted in time the Jewish communities of Europe were. You had towns where Jews had been living for a thousand years, and that really struck hard.

Museum: That brings me to the next question. What has been the reaction to the Jewish focus of your work? Your last three novels, *The Amazing Adventures of Kavalier & Clay*, *The Yiddish Policemen's Union* and *Gentlemen of the Road*, are heavily based on the experience of being Jewish and on Jewish culture. And with *The Yiddish Policemen's Union*, it's in the title; you can't miss it. Has there been any pushback from editors or agents?

MC: No, not at all. The reaction has been much too varied to really summarize. Even among Jewish readers, the reaction has been incredibly varied. Overwhelmingly positive, I would say. But people come at the material from so many different angles. I had people saying about *Kavalier & Clay*, "This brought back a whole world to me" or "This is just like my family." And I also had people saying, "I'm Jewish and I never knew any of this, and I never thought about comic books as being part of my Jewish heritage." Same thing with *Yiddish Policemen's Union*. People come to it bringing a lot of Yiddish knowledge, and people come to it bringing no Yiddish knowledge at all. And then you have all the non-Jewish readers.

Museum: So there are points of accessibility for everyone?
MC: I hope so. I certainly hope so.

Museum: So where does this leave you for your next foray? Are you going to continue along with the sort of fanciful telling of Jewish history?
MC: No, I don't think so. This next novel that I'm going to work on, at least at the moment, will be set in the present, in the recognizable version of consensus reality. I would like to try to incorporate all the work I've done recently into my moving forward. I feel like I've been on this journey of rediscovery and reconnecting to my roots as both an American Jew and as a reader, and I'd like to try to reincorporate both kinds of heritage. With *Yiddish Policemen's Union*, you have this strong immigrant, Yiddish-speaking background and this hardboiled detective novel brought together, and it's kind of the ultimate expression of that rediscovery and that reincorporation of roots. And having done that and at this point feeling quite reconnected to everything that I've ever been as an American, as a Jew, as a writer, as a reader, I feel like I'm going to move forward now and take on this world again, hopefully with a lot of the strength that I've derived from the work that I've been doing most recently.

Totally Unknown in Finland: An Interview with Michael Chabon

Brian Beglin / 2008

From *Sycamore Review* 20.2 (2008). © *Sycamore Review*. Reprinted by permission.

Michael Chabon is the author of six novels, including *The Mysteries of Pittsburgh* (1988), *Wonder Boys* (1995), and *The Amazing Adventures of Kavalier & Clay* (2000), which won the Pulitzer Prize for Fiction in 2001. He is also the author of two short story collections, *A Model World* (1991) and *Werewolves in Their Youth* (1999), and the recent essay collection *Maps and Legends*. He has been a finalist for the PEN/Faulkner Award, the National Book Critics Circle Award, and the *Los Angeles Times* Book Award, and was the guest editor for the *Best American Short Stories* anthology in 2005. He received his MFA from UC-Irvine and currently lives in Berkeley, California. Chabon was the keynote speaker at Purdue University's 77th Annual Literary Awards on April 15, 2008.

Sycamore: *The Mysteries of Pittsburgh* is often called a coming-of-age novel. *The Yiddish Policemen's Union* was just nominated for the Hugo, a science fiction award. How do you react when labels are put on your work?
Chabon: Having that novel nominated for a Hugo Award was actually, in a strange way, like an un-labeling. It had been written, sold, reviewed, and already classified as a somewhat odd but still mainstream literary novel by a somewhat odd but still mainstream literary writer. It didn't come packaged with any real visual clues to tell you don't read this if you don't like science fiction, which is the way science fiction and other genres tend to be coded, to keep the unwary from being somehow contaminated by their presence. It wasn't like that at all. So I view [the nomination] much more as an adop-

tion. The Hugo Award is actually given by readers—fans—so for them to reach out toward the book and embrace it in that way felt like the opposite of labeling.

Sycamore: In *Maps and Legends* you write, "Anything good that I have written has, at some point during its composition, left me feeling uneasy and afraid." You relate writing to building a golem—the novel as this thing that, if you do it right, might just come alive and kill you. Why do you think this danger is so essential to the process?

Chabon: Well, that's what makes it fun. That's why you want to build a golem, because there's always this chance that it might work. But every piece of golem folklore tells you that if they do come to life, they get out of your control. They get beyond your grasp. That's a message and a motif that was picked up by Mary Shelley in *Frankenstein*. It's a very familiar image. And if you tend to think of a novel as being like a golem in some way, you can be assured that if it really comes to life and it gets out into the world and gets loose of you, there's no way of controlling what will happen. That could take all kinds of forms. If you live under a repressive political regime, your words could literally kill you. If you write a novel about family, there's bound to be a member of your family who takes offense at the portrayal of a character even if you weren't thinking of them when you wrote it.

In *Wonder Boys*, the main character's a writer, and he's a big pothead, and he's always sort of creating chaos and disaster for himself. In creating that character, I was thinking of a couple of writing teachers that I've had over the years. But I went to Finland on a trip for the State Department. None of my books had been published in Finland. In fact there was this headline in the biggest newspaper in Helsinki—like the *New York Times* of Finland—and it was my picture and this big headline in Finnish. I said, "What does that say?" And they said, "Yankee Genius Totally Unknown in Finland." So I went on TV while I was there, and the interviewer said, "Mr. Chabon, in your book *Wonder Boys*, your Grady Tripp is smoking many drugs and having many women. How 'bout you?"

So there's that sense as you're writing of, if I say this, if I attribute this kind of behavior to this character, people might think that's me. They might think I do that, they might think I think that. We all do it—when you're reading a novel, you keep flipping back and forth to the author photo, and saying, "Well, he has red hair, and the character has red hair." When you ask, *Can I actually write that? Can I put this in the book and have people know this or think this about me?* . . . that to me is a guarantee that you're on the right track.

Sycamore: Sometimes it works differently. You said you've gotten mail from people wondering where they can find original Joe Kavalier art, or saying they've been to Alaska but never noticed all the Jewish artifacts there.

Chabon: That's a phenomenon that's been creeping up more on me over the years since *Kavalier & Clay*. Because the way *Kavalier & Clay* is written is with this false, omniscient, almost encyclopedic narrator who seems to have full grasp of all the history of the twentieth century, who uses footnotes and always maintains this tone toward the reader that this is all true. That's a very traditional tone for a novelist to adopt, going back to all of those novels that start with the name of the town turned into a dash, or the year is a dash. That promise the novel is making—the false promise—from the very beginning that everything you are about to read actually happened, I used that same approach to *Kavalier & Clay*. And because of that, and because I intertwined real-life characters—Salvador Dalí and Orson Welles—some readers had a hard time sorting out just what was true and what was false. And in fact, that was exactly what I wanted to have happen. I didn't really think it would happen.

I had that experience reading a really good novel called *The Mambo Kings Play Songs of Love* by Oscar Hijuelos. He has these fictional brothers who have a mambo orchestra in New York in the 1950s, and they cut this record. They have this legendary appearance on *I Love Lucy* where they play cousins of Ricky's who come from Cuba. [Hijuelos] describes the whole episode, and at a certain point you start to feel like, "I kind of remember that episode." After I was reading it, I went into a Latin music store in San Francisco and I actually had the thought of wanting to see if they had that Mambo Kings record. And then I was like, "Oh wait, it's fictional. Never mind." I wanted to create that same sense in the reader of *Kavalier & Clay*.

Sycamore: You've talked before about how *Fountain City* was sort of a kitchen sink novel. But your other novels are expansive, too. They take a lot of research, a lot of planning. For you, what's the right balance between research and invention?

Chabon: Doing the research is one of the reasons I like to write novels. I've always been curious about the Khazar Empire and the medieval Caucasus area, or the history of chess, or comic books, or the Yiddish language. These are subjects that I find interesting, and part of the reason I want to write novels about them is because it will give me the chance to educate myself about them. To have that excuse handy, to spend all this time in libraries just going through old magazines and surfing Yiddish websites, is fun. I like to do it.

Of course, it is necessary. You do make very important discoveries in the course of doing research, and often, especially when you're not quite sure what you're looking for, you find things that totally change the course of what you're writing. For example, in *Kavalier & Clay*, I was sitting in the basement of the Bancroft Library on the Cal campus and going through bound back issues of the *New Yorker* magazine in the years that my novel was taking place. Just looking for anything—what movies were playing, and what people were talking about, what they were thinking about. And I found this "Talk of the Town" piece about this researcher for G.E. who was doing research on lightning strikes at the Empire State Building. He was up there every night all summer long with all of his instruments, taking readings. I loved the idea of this lonely guy up there on top of the Empire State Building all night long getting struck by lightning. Eventually that turned out to be just what I needed for *Kavalier & Clay*. [*The novel contains a love scene in the midst of a lightning storm on top of the Empire State Building.*]

That being said, research is also a trap. First of all, you can always justify research to yourself, even when you don't need to. I find this particularly insidious on the Internet; if I have an Internet connection, I try to sever it when I'm actually trying to get work done. The other problem is that the more research you do, the more you start to feel beholden to the facts, and I think that's a really dangerous thing for a fiction writer. The more you know, the more unwilling you become to make things up. You'll find yourself saying things like, "I really need there to have been a green bus on the streets of Savannah, Georgia, in 1938, but everything I've researched tells me all the buses were all yellow." I think one thing about research that has been the hardest for me to learn is how important it is to abandon it.

Sycamore: I read that, in *The Yiddish Policemen's Union*, you purposefully kept your sentences short, almost clipped, compared to your other work. And in *Gentlemen of the Road*, you went the complete opposite direction, sort of consciously overwriting it. Can you talk about your relationship with language, how you approach the sentence- or line-level aspects of craft?

Chabon: I have a natural sentence, the sentence that I hear when I'm trying to tell a story. That sentence tends to be longish and it tends to have a lot of parentheticals and dependent clauses, and I like to use threes. I'll often use three adjectives or give three examples or I'll even use three similes, one right after the other, for the same thing. That is not intentional; it's just the sentence form that feels right to me. But it's also a habit. On second and third draft, I'll go in there and force those sentences to justify their form, justify their existence. I'll look at them and try to break them up and put them into different patterns, hear them in a different way. I had to do that a lot more with *Yiddish Policemen's Union*. It got to the point where I was actually frisking my sentences up against the wall as they emerged. I would write the sentence and pat it down to see whether it was holding anything. I wasn't going to waste time with sentences if they weren't going to work that way, which was more clipped, more compact.

I finished *Yiddish Policemen's Union*, turned it in to my editor, and three days later, I started writing *Gentlemen of the Road*. It was being serialized in the *New York Times*, and they needed it in six or eight weeks. With that, I just took off, turned off all the controls, just let it go. I think the sentences you see in *Gentlemen of the Road*—that's like my naked prose. That's how it comes out naturally, unfettered, because I was writing really fast, trying to get it done. The sentences in that book are very long, very tangled. I like circumlocution. Circumlocution is one of those things we're taught by our English teachers, and rightly so, but I think it's actually capable of very beautiful effects, as well. You force the reader to engage with what it is you aren't saying.

Sycamore: You've written a novel, *The Final Solution*, and done some work in comics and film that required you to write preexisting characters instead of ones entirely of your own creation. How is that a different process?

Chabon: You know, it isn't, really. I really feel that, ultimately, all fiction is fan fiction. Even in creating your own characters, when you make them up entirely out of your own experience, you're not basing them on Buffy or Willow but on actual, real live people. The way that you approach creating characters and telling stories is determined by the reading that you've done, whether it's Dostoevsky or Arthur Conan Doyle. I've always seen writing as an act that puts me into play with the people whose work I love. When I was ten or eleven years old, the first story that I wrote was a Sherlock Holmes story, because I loved Sherlock Holmes. And in writing that first story, I felt as if I were being admitted into a game. That there was this game that all the writers I loved were playing, and I wanted in, and the easiest, readiest way that I could imagine doing that—and I think this is the impulse behind the writing of fan fiction—was by adopting the voice and the characters of Arthur Conan Doyle and writing my own Sherlock Holmes story. The same thing with Sherlock Holmes in *The Final Solution*. I didn't violate any precepts of the canon or the things that are known about Sherlock Holmes. But I still tried to fully invest the character, and tried to approach it as if I were making him up for the very first time.

I'm really still trying to get in on the game. All writers are in dialogue with each other. In the Buffyverse or the *Star Trek* universe, there is this sort of shared, collective enterprise going on. To me, literature is just a bigger, broader shared universe.

Michael Chabon: Streams in a River

Locus / 2008

From *Locus: The Magazine of the Science Fiction and Fantasy Field* August 2008: 7, 60–61. ©
Locus. Reprinted by permission.

Michael Chabon was born May 24, 1963, in Washington, DC, and raised in
a utopian community in Columbia, Maryland. He attended the University
of Pittsburgh, receiving a BA in 1984 in English Literature, then an MFA at
the University of California at Irvine; his master's thesis became his first
novel, bestselling coming-of-age story *The Mysteries of Pittsburgh* (1988).
Other novels include *Wonder Boys* (1995), Pulitzer Prize winner *The Amazing Adventures of Kavalier & Clay* (2000), Mythopoeic Award–winning YA
Summerland (2002), and historical mystery *The Final Solution* (2004). *The
Yiddish Policemen's Union* (2007), which combines the alternate history and
hardboiled detective genres, won a Nebula, a Locus Award, and was a finalist for the British Science Fiction Award and the Edgar Award. It is currently
a Hugo nominee and a Sidewise Award finalist. His Fritz Leiber–influenced
historical adventure *Gentlemen of the Road* (2007) was serialized in the *New
York Times Magazine* before book publication, and once had the working
title *Jews with Swords*. He has published two story collections, *A Model
World and Other Stories* (1991) and *Werewolves in Their Youth* (1999), and
essay collection *Maps and Legends* (2008). He writes a regular column for
Details magazine.

Chabon edited anthologies *McSweeney's Mammoth Treasury of Thrilling
Tales* (2003) and *McSweeney's Enchanted Chamber of Astonishing Stories*
(2004), and *Best American Short Stories: 2005* (2005), the latter notable for
its inclusion of several genre stories. He edited comic book anthologies *The
Amazing Adventures of the Escapist* Volumes 1 and 2 (2004–5), and six-issue
comic mini-series *The Escapists* (2006), featuring his character from *The
Amazing Adventures of Kavalier & Clay*.

He lives in Berkeley, California with his wife, mystery writer Ayelet Waldman (married 1993), and their four children.

"I didn't have any hesitation about drawing on different traditions in trying
to write *The Yiddish Policemen's Union*; on the contrary, that was one of the
things that was exciting about doing it. When I realized it was going to be
both a hardboiled detective novel and alternate history, that was part of the
reason I wanted to write it! I was curious to see how that would come out.

"I remember reading things which blended genres that way. Isaac
Asimov's Lucky Starr novels—those are detective stories. (I liked them at
the time.) And Larry Niven did 'Gil the Arm.' *Blade Runner* was noir and SF
at the same time. So it was far from the case that I thought, 'Oh nobody's
ever done this.' There was a tradition and I was fully aware I was drawing on
it. I guess for me the new wrinkle (if there was one) was going to be the Jewish subject matter, bringing that in as a kind of key third element.

"I heard Yiddish a lot when I was growing up, though I was kept at arm's
length from it by relatives who didn't really want me to know what they were
saying most of the time. In the early '90s I found the phrasebook *Say It in
Yiddish* in a bookstore, and I was really mystified and entranced by it. If I
wanted to goof off a little, I would just pick it up and page through it.

"All phrasebooks are inherently funny, because they have this kind of ab-
surdist, dadaist quality. Often it's hard to imagine real-life applications for
the ready-made phrases that have been chosen for you. Then there's this
further element that it was Yiddish, and premised on the idea that you could
take this eminently practical book somewhere else and use it. And yet there
was no clue, on the jacket or in an introduction, where you would take it!
Even in Crown Heights, Brooklyn, there's no post office staffed entirely by
Yiddish speakers where you need to speak Yiddish in order to buy postage
stamps. It was so richly detailed in-between the lines, it implied an incredibly detailed place. It was like the mysterious book in the Borges story that
seems to imply an entire universe within its pages—a magic artifact of a
nonexistent place.

"So I wrote this essay where I tried both to guess (unsuccessfully) at the
author's intentions and speculate on possible destinations to which he could
have taken this phrasebook if history had come out a little differently. And
in passing, I dwelt briefly on this actual proposal I had read about to permit
Jewish refugees to settle in Alaska before the Second World War (it didn't
get very far).

"Afterwards, the more I thought about it the more I felt that might be an interesting place to set a novel. I also had a perverse reaction . . . . There was a certain amount of criticism of my essay among the small world of Yiddish enthusiasts, those who are still passionate about it. They had an online forum where they discussed Yiddish, and some of the members were annoyed or irritated or outright offended by this essay because they felt the fundamental implication was that Yiddish is a dead language, and that's what makes this phrasebook funny and poignant.

"*I* was saying it's funny and poignant not because Yiddish is a dead language but because there is no such place and I wished there were—I wished I could go there and see it for myself. But having offended them, I decided to see if I could offend them a little more. My book *Gentlemen of the Road* is partly about the Khazars. The history of the Khazars is so secret, not only is it not generally known that there was this quasi-Jewish kingdom in the Caucasus region for a good four or five hundred years from the early Middle Ages, but there's so little known even by those writers who *do* know about them. There are a few artifacts and a few mentions in the works of some of the great Arab travelers of the time, and that's about it. There's very little information, even though they were this reputedly great civilization. That was an open invitation to me as a novelist, because that's the optimal situation: where you can get away with making up as much as you feel like. (I tried to be faithful to the historical record, such as it is.)

"I had been tossing around this idea for a long time, thinking maybe it could be a movie, a novel . . . I didn't know what it could be. Then I got this offer to do a serialized novel for the *New York Times* Sunday Magazine; they said to keep it short (those are pulp restrictions) but not what to write. They just said, 'Would you like to fill this space in our magazine for fifteen weeks?' That felt like the perfect approach. It would force me to structure and plot it out in a way I'd been unwilling to do up until that point. I had a chapter-by-chapter outline before I started, and I stuck to it pretty closely. And since they wanted the whole thing done before they published it, I didn't have to write it by the seat of my pants.

"Over the years, I probably have read equally in sword and sorcery with actual magic content and more straightforward historical adventure. With this one, I felt it was about the partnership between these two guys and the fact that they are con men to a certain degree. They plied their trade in a world where the rules of physics apply, and that's what they had to contend against. If recourse to magic and sorcery were possible, it would make them and their challenges less appealing.

"I'm not religious at all, and I never have been. I'm an agnostic, at most.

(Although I could see keeping kosher, as long as it didn't oblige me to believe in God. I'd be fine with that.) I grew up in a household that was moderately observant, in a 1970s suburban Maryland kind of way. I had the bar mitzvah and we went to services. But whatever it takes to be a believer, I never had that quality.

"I did grow away from my sense of Jewish identity, primarily through my twenties. Then in my late twenties, when I had just started to try to find my way back to it, I met my wife Ayelet Waldman, who is also Jewish. Together we've kind of gone about the project of building a Jewish identity, as a couple and a family with our children. It's easy to do stuff like that in Berkeley, to forge a new spiritual and cultural identity on your own terms. That's what living here is all about. Everybody's doing that in one way or another.

"I am strongly identified as a Jewish American writer, and Jewish American in general, and much more confident and sure about that than at any prior time in my life. There's an essay in my nonfiction collection *Maps and Legends* about how I came to realize recently that as I was going through that process—turning my back on being Jewish and then, in a sense, rediscovering it and reincorporating it into my life—that process almost exactly paralleled what happened to me with science fiction, fantasy, and detective mystery fiction as well.

"As I was turning my back on Judaism and going out into the world to try to find a more universal kind of identity, I was doing the same thing as a reader and a writer. Up to a certain point in my teens or early twenties my writing, if not outright SF or fantasy, was always on the borders. There were discoveries I needed to make in terms of prose style and creating characters, psychology of characters, that I don't think I could have made as quickly and as easily on a steady diet of science fiction and fantasy. I needed to go out there and immerse myself in literature as a whole.

"It's less true of other art forms, but for some reason with writers in particular we want to know where to stick them, where to *shelve* them. There's a general tendency in the world to force people to assume positions that are much more rigid than what comes naturally to them. Once you make what you think is a choice that's going to empower you in some way, often it turns out somewhere down the line that it turned into a trap: you were actually closing out a lot of options to yourself without realizing it. I think there comes a moment for all artists where they have to look around and realize that's what happened, and try to figure out where they made those choices.

"I'm a reader first and foremost, and the choices I make as a writer tend to reflect the choices I make as a reader. So when I'm trying to get going on a project I always ask myself, 'Is this something I would want to read?'—something I wish I could read, something that seems to be missing on the shelf.

"A standard view of literary critics is that plot is an inherent weakness. That's a vestigial holdover from the Modernist movement in the early part of the twentieth century, where painting abandoned figuration, music abandoned harmony, poetry abandoned meter, and to a certain degree fiction abandoned plot. Plot in fiction had become fairly conventionalized, and it probably *did* feel like something that needed to be loosened up, reexamined, questioned, challenged. I think plot, unchecked, does weaken the power of a work of fiction. If a novel is overly in service to its plot, there's always a diminishment of character and psychology. Plot and character are in an inverse proportional relationship to each other, for the most part. In my own work, I try to find a balance point. Some of Henry James's work is finely plotted. I think *The Turn of the Screw* is his most perfect book, and it does find that balance: character is illuminated by the plot in an ideal way that we could all aspire to.

"For me, it's not that I feel writing conventional (or whatever you want to call it) fiction was a mistake. The novel I'm working on now is straight-ahead, naturalistic, but it's informed by the writing I've been doing in the past seven to nine years. Ultimately they do all derive from the same source: stories being told around the fire, stories of the Dreamtime. So they're just streams in a very broad river.

"There's always somebody ready and waiting to slap a label on. People love labels, and they like labeling other people with them. If you make yourself (in a sense) vulnerable to being labeled, people are happy to do that but not to remove that label or let you have others put on you. Which is weird, because it's human nature to be multivalent, to have conflicting impulses and elements in our nature. And people, generally speaking, either resist labels or can be easily labeled in all kinds of different ways without implying any kind of conflict or contradiction.

"The name that springs most readily to my lips is Ursula K. Le Guin. To me she's one of the great American writers of the late twentieth century and now the twenty-first, *period.* But for all the recognition that she has received, the fact that she came so powerfully out of the science fiction world has been a liability for her in terms of getting the ultimate recognition. (Though one doesn't have that sense, with her, of a writer struggling to break out.)

"I worked to actively solicit the material in the two 'pulp' anthologies I edited—*McSweeney's Mammoth Treasury of Thrilling Tales* and *McSwee-*

ney's Enchanted Chamber of Astonishing Stories—while in *The Best American Short Stories* I was more of a judge. Ultimately, I could only rely on my own taste as a reader, and that was it. I couldn't even guarantee it had any kind of integrity or coherence. I was just going to be reading through this pile of over 200 short stories, trying to pick the ones that pleased me the most. Who am I to say these are the *best* stories?

"But I kept pushing the series editor to send me more stuff culled from a broader range of places, and when I felt I wasn't getting enough of that I went out looking on my own, checking out websites, genre work, various anthologies. I wanted *noir*, fantasy, science fiction. . . . So I suppose in that sense I did have a kind of agenda at work.

"In some ways, I think the second McSweeney's book is stronger than the first. In those I wanted to do two things. One: I had this feeling I could not be the only mainstream fiction writer out there who loved some genre in which he or she was not actively working, possibly for reasons of fear that it wouldn't be taken seriously, or that the opportunity had never arisen. If that was the case, I could maybe go to a bunch of people I think are great writers who are totally not identified with any of the standard genres, and see if they wanted to try something. To go to Rick Moody and ask, 'Would you like to write a science fiction story?' and have him immediately say, 'Yeah, I've always wanted to and in fact I have this idea...' I got that reaction almost universally, even from people who declined to participate for whatever reason.

"The other side of it was feeling that there are plenty of distinctions between genres, but the distinctions also get pushed outward into extra-literary things where the writers themselves get kept apart. I wanted to just push writers together who otherwise would probably not find themselves in the same anthology, and see what happened.

"And I got a Moorcock story! He was one of the writers I was most passionate about at a certain time in my life. I was a huge Elric fan, I read all the Jerry Cornelius books, every DAW paperback edition. I thought he was *god* back then, so to get to meet him as I have in the past several years . . . . He's so sweet and fun to talk to. It's still exciting.

"I want to write another novel for younger readers and I know what that's going to be, but I just felt that it had been since *Wonder Boys* in the early '90s that I had written a novel set in consensus reality—modern-day America—and I missed it. I was making things hard on myself for a long time, in that with everything I needed to say in the work I would have to stop and think, 'Well, did they have those back then?' Whether it was New York in the 1930s and '40s or in an imaginary Yiddish-speaking territory in the United States or in the Caucasus Mountains in the year 950, there was always a sense that everything I was seeing and hearing around me in my daily life—grist for the mill for writers—I was having to put through all of these filters, because there were no cars or no phones back then. It's stressful.

"So it's pleasurable for me to be working on this novel set now, here in Oakland and Berkeley. I love this place so much and it turns out that I actually know a lot about it. I understand it, and to be able to just put that understanding directly into practice in the work of fiction I'm writing is actually a relief. Nevertheless, I think a lot of the same concerns, themes, motifs, and even to some degree conventions, that I have been exploring in my recent work will find their way into this book.

"I'll also be doing another volume of my nonfiction. I have a column in *Details* magazine every month, and over the years I've written a lot of other essays that have to do with aspects of my life as a man—a father, a son and a husband. I'm going to try to collect all that into some kind of shape that works as a book."

On Comics, Genres, and Styles: A Conversation with Michael Chabon

Victoria Ramirez and Patrick Murphy / 2009

From *Weber: The Contemporary West* 27.1 (Fall 2010): 2–16. Reprinted by permission.

Michael Chabon is a much sought-after writer and a man with a busy sched-ule. Thus, when Chabon agreed to be the featured author for Weber State University's National Undergraduate Literature Conference (NULCO) in April 2009, and further graciously agreed to make time to meet with me, I was delighted. I felt honored to be conducting the interview, though daunt-ed, too, as I was only slightly familiar with Chabon's work. His novel *Won-der Boys* (1995) had been made into a feature-length movie and I'd enjoyed watching that immensely. But as for his other books . . .

That's where Patrick Murphy enters the story. After our MA class one day, I mentioned that I would be interviewing Chabon, and Patrick almost bounced off the ceiling. He knew all about Chabon, having been at the 2004 Eisner Awards ceremony (the highest-level industry honors—it's like the Oscars, but for comics) at the San Diego Comic-Con where Chabon was to give the keynote address. Patrick is, like Chabon, an openly admitted comic book fan. I couldn't resist the obvious: Patrick Murphy had to be part of the interview team!

Chabon is a writer of diverse interests and passions, though central to all these is the act of writing—and reading. His passion won him a Pulit-zer Prize in 2001 for his novel *The Amazing Adventures of Kavalier & Clay* (2000), the story of two Brooklyn cousins who create a popular comic book series in the 1940s. This is a book Patrick Murphy highly recommends, not only to anyone who has anything more than a passing interest in comic books, but also to any reader wanting to catch the hardships and frustra-tions of Jewish Americans before, during, and after World War II. Not only a tour de force in itself, *Kavalier & Clay* demonstrates a truth about Chabon's opus: the author has many chops and can write in diverse voices, genres, styles.

Thus, his first novel, *The Mysteries of Pittsburgh* (1988), is a coming-of-age tale that draws on Chabon's years in Pittsburgh, where he attended college. A favorite story about this book is that it was actually a thesis for an MFA in fiction, and was submitted, unbeknownst to Chabon, to a publisher by his thesis advisor, who landed Chabon a lucrative publication deal. His second novel, *Wonder Boys* (1995), offers readers a look into the world of literary conferences and features the trippy character Grady Tripp. Without revealing too much of the story, let me just say everything in the book about literary conventions is pretty much true, as is all that stuff about writer's block.

The following interview reveals a few of the more interesting facts about Chabon as writer. He is considered a "genre" novelist, a term I suspect Chabon resists to a degree, not because there is no truth to the label, but because any narrowing of a writer's potential (that is, pigeon-holing for any sake other than the creation of stories fun to read) is of minimal concern to him. Chabon strikes me as a pragmatist of his own imaginings, confident that the best books from his mind surely are those that offer dang good stories, regardless of genre. Time and again Chabon has waxed eloquent on the truism that no one genre is inherently more valuable or literary than another. This point looms large as he has won five genre awards, and for *The Yiddish Policemen's Union* (2007) received both the prestigious Hugo and Nebula science fiction awards. Chabon's genre nimbleness further revealed itself when he published his novella, *The Final Solution* (2004), a quirky tale bound to delight any Sherlock Holmes fan. This story also reveals one of Chabon's enduring themes: Jewishness, which makes its way into much of his work.

As if publishing *The Yiddish Policemen's Union* in 2007 wasn't enough, that year Chabon also came out with *Gentlemen of the Road*, a swashbuckling mini-saga on which Kerouac *et al.* have not a thing. Again, this early medieval tale exemplifies the dictum Chabon writes by: let the spirit, and your own interests, move you, and you'll produce passionate writing that entertains others. In addition to the novels listed above, Chabon has written a young-adult book, *Summerland* (2002); he's published two short story collections, *A Model World* (1991) and *Werewolves in Their Youth* (1999); and Chabon's essay collections include *Maps and Legends* (2008) and *Manhood for Amateurs* (2009).

In his address to the gathered student scholars attending Weber State University's National Undergraduate Literature Conference, Chabon read a four-part essay titled "From Fandom to Legoland." His address started with his childhood aspirations to organize a comic book club, a failure with haunting reverberations, and how his quest for acceptance ended with his family, his own fan club. All four parts have since been printed in his recent book of essays, *Manhood for Amateurs*, as "The Loser's Club," "Surefire Lines," "To the Legoland Station," and "The Amateur Family." Within his NULC address, and within the proceeding interview, one theme rings clear: Michael Chabon is not only a writer but, additionally, a husband and father. This is the secret to how Chabon continues to entertain and delight his audience: beyond his quick writing and deep wit there is an underlying voice that is eternally speaking with a resonant understanding of the connectivity that defines us as human.

Ramirez: Michael Chabon, I just wanted to say that Patrick is my graduate student, and one day he was talking about you, just by-the-by, and I said, "Oh that's the dude coming to the conference," and he got all excited. Patrick is a real fan of yours, and so I asked him to be in on the conversation.
Murphy: This is for me and my school.
Michael Chabon: I thought you were going to say this is for two hundred points.

Murphy: I am a high school English teacher. For my junior class *The Amazing Adventures of Kavalier & Clay* is on my student reading list.
Michael Chabon: Thank you.

Murphy: If one of my students were considering reading this novel, what advice would you have for her and what should she get out of the experience?
Michael Chabon: I would advise her to buy two copies and give one to a friend. I don't think I can really answer that. I would analogize it to being in the room when someone picks up one of my books, or being in a bookstore. Once or twice I've been in a store when someone was walking over to a table that had my books and picked up a copy of something I'd written. You feel an incredible sense of embarrassment and dread and anticipation mixed with the certainty that they are going to put the book down and walk away, which in fact is what's happened every time I've seen it in a bookstore. So that position of being present as someone is beginning to read your book or has been required to read your book is kind of a nauseating feeling.

Murphy: So what's the lesson that they can bring into their lives?

Michael Chabon: I don't have any idea. I'm not trying to shirk the question. More than anything else I would like someone to find the experience of reading that book, or any of my books, pleasurable and enjoyable. It's hard to have that experience when you feel like it's obligatory. Obligatory pleasure is never as pleasurable. So I wouldn't want to be in there trying to say, "You know what I need you to learn from reading this, or I know what I expect you to get out of reading this." That would feel very intrusive to me. I don't want to intrude. I am happy to be there at the other end when the reader comes out of the book and says, "I have these questions. I wonder about this, why was it like that, how does this work?" At that point I am much more comfortable being involved in the conversation, but I don't feel comfortable being involved in the conversation before somebody has even begun the book.

Ramirez: So, you'd advise the person, the student, to buy two copies to give it to a buddy. Would that be so that they could talk about it?

Michael Chabon: No, so that I could get double the worth.

Ramirez: [*Laughs*] Okay.

Michael Chabon: I'm just kidding about that.

Ramirez: Because at that age they are not going to know a lot of other people who've read that book. You have no one else that you can really talk to about what's in it.

Michael Chabon: Right. It's very flattering to learn that a book you wrote is being taught in a class. It's exciting because I realize that once that has happened—once that begins to happen—it really does ensure a longer life for what you have written. And once things begin to be taught at the university level, they become part of a much longer-lasting conversation. [At first] it occurs at the newspaper review level. That's a conversation. Typically it doesn't last that long.

Murphy: I teach a science fiction literature class for juniors and that's where I assign *The Amazing Adventures of Kavalier & Clay*. And I'll probably end up putting in *The Yiddish Policemen's Union* because it does ask those "what if" questions. As an old "Marvel zombie," I was excited when a *What If?* comic would come out, because it gave you ideas about possibilities. And that's what's so good about *The Yiddish Policemen's Union*. But you go from genre to genre and you are talking about breaking down genres in some of

your essays because if it's good, it's good, and if it's bad, it's bad. Do you feel you are reinforcing genres, or do you feel you are breaking them down?
Michael Chabon: Neither. I guess I feel much more like I'm just playing with them and trying them on in a sense. And drawing on the conventions, the traditions and the history of various genres as a source of narrative ideas in my writing. I'm not really thinking about breaking them down or anything like that. They're just useful to me.

Murphy: Are there any genres that you wanted to write in but haven't yet?
Michael Chabon: It might be fun to try writing a western someday. I love westerns, but I don't know if I'll ever get around to it. It's not like I have a checklist of genres, and I say, "Okay, I did fantasies, I did hardboiled detective, now western is next." I wouldn't do it just to do it. I would only do it if I got an idea for a story that felt like it could be best told using the framework or the conventions of a western, and playing with them. If such a story doesn't ever occur to me, then I won't do it, even though I love westerns and it would probably be fun to write one. For me, it's just a matter of realizing that I could write in various genres, that there is a whole crucial part of my lifelong experience as a reader of which I was not really availing myself as a writer, and that seemed wrong. It seemed stupid and foolish. I had just drawn this sort of *cordon sanitaire* around my work and said, "Well, I can't write science fictions, I can't write fantasies, I can't do any of those things I love to read because if I do, I'm not writing serious literature." At some point I just realized that was both foolish and hypocritical and wasn't serving me well. Furthermore, it didn't reflect my deepest motivations for wanting to become a writer in the first place. So, I lifted that barrier and said, I'm just going to write whatever I want to write, whatever kind of narrative I need to tell the stories that I'm trying to tell. If it turns out to be hardboiled detective fiction, so be it. I love hardboiled detective fiction. Why shouldn't I write hardboiled detective fiction? But, again, not just to show that I can, or as a pure exercise in genre, but because that was the narrative solution to trying to tell the story that I wanted to tell about this imaginary Yiddish-speaking homeland in Alaska.

I needed to present that to the reader, and it was a totally unfamiliar world, unfamiliar environment. The reader needed to have someone as a kind of guide who knew the place well. Who understood its inner mechanics and the way that its social structures worked, and all the things that a detective understands. That was the perfect main character for that book, because a detective implies the city that he operates in, the way Marlowe implies Los Angeles, Sam Spade implies San Francisco, and Sherlock Holmes implies London. So if I created my detective I could use him to imply the world I was trying to create. It was at that moment where the important decision that I made several years ago to let myself write whatever I felt like writing—whatever kind of books that I love to read, to allow that love to feed my writing—kicked in and said, "Okay, great, you have a detective novel."

Murphy: As an author, you kind of identify yourself with Edgar Rice Burroughs, who wrote in just every genre, though he was only known for the Tarzan jungle stuff. But Burroughs did science fiction, he did westerns, and he was a WWII war correspondent.

Michael Chabon: Well, I think it's different. I love Edgar Rice Burroughs. He was one of my favorite writers when I was young and I still read him now. In fact, I'm working on a rewrite for a screenplay for the *John Carter of Mars* movie that Disney is doing. So, I am very connected to Burroughs. But that's different. He was writing for market. That is why he wrote in different genres. He wrote where he thought he could sell. There were western magazines, so he wrote westerns. There were fantasy adventure magazines, like *Argosy*, and he wrote for those markets. The same with Robert E. Howard. He wrote not just the Conan stories he is famous for, but boxing stories, sea stories, western frontier stories, even humor. Those guys wrote in different genres because they got paid a penny a word, and they just needed to hit as many markets as they possibly could. All hail their incredible versatility that they could do that, but I think that's very different. That's not about freedom so much as it is about necessity. When you are a Robert E. Howard and you're writing a boxing story, it's because you have to, because you need to make money and there is a boxing market. There is a fight magazine and they take stories about boxing, so you aim a story. You might even take one of your barbarian stories and recast it, and turn the sword into boxing gloves. They did that kind of thing all the time and vice versa. That's about tailoring your abilities to the market. In my case, it is about opening up my fiction to incorporate as many of the influences and passions that I have had in my life, and not to have that sort of invisible barrier. It keeps out the stuff that has typically been considered unliterary.

Ramirez: I look at this as coming to the awareness of what authors like Vonnegut and Pynchon and other mainstream literary writers successfully do in their work, and nobody calls them science fiction novels when, actually, they are.

Michael Chabon: Exactly. That's something I definitely also want to resist because there is this move made by critics, and Cormac McCarthy is another example, where if a writer is generally accepted to be a genius or a literary master, and writes a work of science fiction, it's not science fiction because it was written by the literary master, it's literature. Even McCarthy's *The Road* is not science fiction, or Vonnegut at a certain point, though he started out writing in the pulp science fiction magazines. At a certain point his status was altered and thereafter everything he did was simply literature and was no longer regarded as coming out of the tradition that it was so obviously coming out of. It's like we make this dispensation, instead of giving the credit to the genre itself, and saying, "Look what incredible power Thomas Pynchon or Margaret Atwood have derived from the tradition that they're working in, that they are a part of." It's the same tradition that Ursula K. Le Guin and Isaac Asimov and others belong to. Instead of saying, "Look at the incredible power that they derive from the tradition they are working in," we say, "How amazing it is that such a great writer can make a great book even out of materials as worthless as those in science fiction."

Murphy: Yeah, well, you look at Philip K. Dick's *The Man in the High Castle*. It has the same sort of "what if" situation as your book, *The Yiddish Policemen's Union*. I really hope your book doesn't get shoved in a science fiction closet and not taken seriously.

Michael Chabon: No. I think I was fairly safe from that happening just because I was already sort of in the box with the literary writers.

Murphy: Philip K. Dick didn't win a Pulitzer.

Michael Chabon: Exactly. He worked his way up definitely from the bottom of the literary pile, from the pulp world and the short magazine fiction world. But I didn't want to be accorded that special dispensation. I didn't want to be viewed as a literary writer who was dabbling in science fiction. So when that book, *Policemen's Union*, won the Hugo Award and the Nebula Award, I couldn't make it to the Hugo Award ceremony unfortunately, but I went to the Nebula Award ceremony. I wanted to be there, I wanted to show that I was proud to be given that award, that I didn't consider it to be a lesser accomplishment. With the Hugo, I couldn't make it but I sent a speech. The first words of my speech were, "I am a science fiction writer." For me, what I don't want is to have one label. I'm happy to have multiple labels. I'm happy to wear multiple labels. I will accept science fiction writer, gladly. Mystery writer, literary writer, Jewish American writer, there are all kinds of labels that you can put on my work and I will take them all as long as they fit. But I think the death comes from when you get one label and that's the only label you are allowed to have and you get stuck with that one label. That's something I would definitely fight against and resist.

Ramirez: I am going to ask a technical question. In *Wonder Boys*, the first book that I read of yours, I noted what I'll call the "Chabonian pause." That is, a character speaks a line which is then followed in the same paragraph by explanation or digression from the narrator, and then ends with one more line spoken by the character. I see this technique in almost all of your books. How and when did you develop this?

Michael Chabon: I don't know if I remember anymore why I started doing it.

Ramirez: Do you remember when? Was it in your first novel?

Michael Chabon: I don't know if it's in *The Mysteries of Pittsburgh* or not. I'm certainly aware of it. "It feels good" would be the only real explanation. I suppose part of the idea is that a lot can happen between the first word of dialogue and the last. It's a way of showing that your entire understanding of the world can change between opening words of what it is you have to say and the final words of what it is you have to say. So that's part of it. Sometimes I use it as a pacing thing where, if the dialogue has been kind of flowing pretty quick and snappy, I want to slow things down and arrest the progress, just to let everyone catch up. There's also a rhythmic thing. I want to make sure the reader is with me, is paying attention still, that you're not reading so quickly that you can't even remember what was at the beginning of the paragraph that you are reading now. If I have a concluding line of dialogue at the end of a paragraph about twelve lines long, and you don't remember what that is the follow-up of, even though it was just twelve lines ago, I think you are reading too fast. I just want to make sure that you are getting everything; that you are really paying attention to everything. I think it's a way of forcing, in a sense, the reader to keep paying attention, to suspend the resolution of the dialogue long enough to make you go, "Wait, wowowowowo, what did he say? Oh, right, okay. These two pieces actually go together." I think there can be a little bit of suspense. There is also a little bit of, "Well, what is he going to say?" If he opens up by saying, "I wish I could help you but . . ." and then this elaboration follows, then how is that going to conclude? Maybe it's going to be that he says, "Okay, alright, I will come and help you." Sometimes, also, I'm using it to reflect the state of mind in the character. A sense of hesitation, or cogitation where the character doesn't really know what he or she thinks, and is thinking it over. So the character, like many of us, starts talking before he or she really knows what he or she wants to say. So we start out and then there is actually a certain amount of hesitation or a thought process takes place. What you end up saying might be very different than what you started saying. Sometimes I just want to show how the character gets from the initial refusal to help, to finally, at the end of it, agreeing to help. I guess there are a lot of reasons and to be honest, I don't think about it, I just do it. I probably noticed it in Gabriel García Márquez first; it's something that he does.

Murphy: The way you described it for controlling the pacing is like paneling in comics, where the artist has the complete control to slow down time, to speed up time. It's almost taking this visual medium and putting it into a literary medium. It's interesting.

Michael Chabon: Right, there is an element of control. You're always trying to modulate. I want it to be pleasurable. I want the reader to be able to get caught up in it and to feel like you're being moved along, buoyed along, and you want to keep turning pages and find out what happens. On the other hand, I write on the sentence level. I write each sentence one at a time. Each sentence is considered and worked over. I don't let that sentence go until I feel like it is doing just what it is supposed to be doing. I'm trying to balance the pacing and the question of narrative drive, of what is pushing the reader through. I'm trying to always balance that with the sense of, "Slow down, think about this, look at this." Have you ever actually looked at a mustache before and noticed what weird things mustaches are? Let me just get you to do that by describing this guy's mustache right here so that you stop and think about mustaches for three seconds, and then you can go on. There is always this tension between the drive of the plot and the narrative and pacing. Because you are trying to do two things: you are trying to tell a good story and you are trying to get the reader to see the world again for the first time in a different way. Those things are always in tension with each other. Sometimes you lose control over that. Sometimes things start moving too quickly and the reader is just blowing through, which can be a good thing. And sometimes you slow things down too much and the reader starts to lose that sense of drive and their energy begins to flag.

Murphy: *Maps and Legends.* The essay that caught my interest in *Maps and Legends* was "Kids' Stuff." I was actually at the 2004 Eisner Award Ceremony where you delivered this essay as a keynote address.

Michael Chabon: In a slightly altered form.

Murphy: In this address you basically stood before all the top comic book industry professionals and told them that current trends were destructive to comic books, as they were alienating a younger audience while catering to a narrowing field of aging readers. It was basically pulling a Brando, going to the Academy Awards and giving a speech on how Hollywood has decayed over the years.

Michael Chabon: But, I didn't refuse my award.

Murphy: Did you receive any backlash from that speech, and how have comics changed since 2004?

Michael Chabon: I did, definitely. I heard, maybe even read online, some people that were ticked off by what I said.

Murphy: Was it fans or professionals?

Michael Chabon: Professionals. Either because they just disagreed or because they felt attacked.

Murphy: I was behind that velvet rope with my buddies, and back there we were just cheering you on.

Michael Chabon: I felt there was more agreement than disagreement in the reaction that I did see. I go to my comic shop, Comic Relief in Berkeley, and they have a whole table now of comics for kids, all kids of cool stuff. From superhero stuff that is aimed at kids to much more alternative independent kind of stuff, even self-published things that are all aimed at young readers. I feel like there is definitely more of that now. My daughter is fourteen and I used to take her into comic book stores with me when she was little. There would be this one little row at the bottom where they would have a couple of DC comics for kids, and Archie stuff or whatever, and maybe *Bone*, and that would be it. I would have to hide her eyes from seeing all this other completely wildly inappropriate stuff, or stuff she would be attracted to because it was *Wonder Woman*, or whatever. But then she would pick it up and the content was totally inappropriate for her. And now I still have young kids; I have a six-year-old son, and now, when we go into a comic shop, I say, "Go over there, there's all kinds of cool stuff over there." So I am not taking the credit for the change, but it was an irresistible argument in the sense that all I was saying was, "Hook 'em early." Don't forget that these kids are going to grow up to be people with disposable incomes, and you want to get them now. So give them stuff they'll like.

Murphy: I think there was a very tender moment at the Eisner Awards when Will Eisner came up right after your address and said with great verve, "Well, now I want to go out and write comics." We all cheered. That was really an amazing moment because you could see that it was something that inspired him.

Michael Chabon: It meant a lot to me, definitely. He was a great guy; he was always very kind to me.

Ramirez: Going back to *Maps and Legends*, one of the articles I read with focus was on *The Road*. I'm teaching this course on Cormac McCarthy so I'm always looking for something good to read. It made me think of this question for you. McCarthy is an author—and I'm going to make a supposition here—like yourself, whose opus centers on relationships between males. I get the sense that a strong theme for McCarthy is, for want of a better term, masculinist in nature, meaning that his most pervasive themes concern themselves with American men and violence. Violence that is promoted through lack of kind fathering or the absence of a protective father. I invoke the carrier of fire you mentioned in your essay. Anyway, you feature men not so much violent as flawed, who often don't have fathers, or have awkward relationships with a father, such as Zelickman in *Gentlemen of the Road*. Would you say your representation of male characters overlaps to a degree with that of McCarthy?

Michael Chabon: When you put it that way, it sounds pretty plausible. Yeah. I mean, I've never really thought about that before.

Ramirez: Because in *Gentlemen of the Road*, you have two men, one of them is very difficult and the other not so bad at times. But there's great love, tenderness, and respect outside of any kind of romantic implication. So, they're men capable of loving and nurturing. That's what I see there and in other places, such as in *The Final Solution*. The difficult Holmes has this incredibly protective and tender side. I see that in various spots throughout your work. And you have characters whose fathers are absent or whatever, like Grady Tripp's in *Wonder Boys*.

Michael Chabon: I think McCarthy is a writer, especially in *Blood Meridian*, one of my favorite novels, who has a much bleaker, unsparing, less hopeful view of human behavior than I do.

Ramirez: In that book, though, it's interesting because it is such a violently written book. It was very difficult for me to read it. One of my students urged me to do so, so I did. Of course, the writing is beautiful. What I came away with, and that's where I arrived at my theory—because the Judge in *Blood Meridian* is the epitome of all the violence—is the pervasiveness of senseless violence.

Michael Chabon: I think it goes way back in American literature. I think part of what makes him so remarkable is how his work resonates with the classic themes of the American literature ideal like *Huck Finn*, and back to Cooper and the captivity narratives. I mean, there is something that is just so Faulkner. There's something so unmistakably primal. I first read, I think, *All the Pretty Horses*, then I read *Blood Meridian*. You just get that charge when you pick up McCarthy's books and start reading. They've got such a charge, and that charge goes back to the earliest kinds of narratives we produced in this country. It's like baseball. When you go to a baseball game you're tapping immediately into this really central, primal kind of American narrative.

Murphy: I'll go back to the geek stuff. Your character The Escapist from *Kavalier & Clay* was eventually turned into an actual comic book, printed by Dark Horse comics. You've had an impressive list of artists working on that comic, including comic legends like Bill Sienkiewicz, Gene Colan, and Will Eisner. Living or dead, who is the artist you would most like to see work on The Escapist and why?

Michael Chabon: Jack Kirby. I don't have to think about that one for a second. No doubt. One of my great regrets is that I didn't start working on *Kavalier & Clay* until Kirby had already been dead for maybe a year or so before I started writing the book. If he had just held on a little longer, I knew people. I knew somebody who knew Marv Wolfman, and Marv Wolfman put me in touch with Gil Kane, and I'm sure he would have been able to hook me up with Kirby, too. So I would have had the opportunity to meet him, which I never did.

Murphy: But you got Eisner.

Michael Chabon: Yes. Eisner, Lee, and Kane, those were my three primary sources.

Murphy: Didn't Eisner call you a "Fan Boy"?

Michael Chabon: Yes, so I was told afterward.

Murphy: He said that in an aside to his wife. Which is a compliment.

Michael Chabon: Yeah. It was funny because it was in a way not really true at that time. In a sense, yes, I had been a "Fan Boy" of comics, but I was actually kind of reconnecting, trying to get back into the world of comics. At the point I was talking to him, "Fan Boy" was an inaccurate term in the sense that I was not really; that wasn't where I was coming from when I wanted to meet and talk with him. The truth is, I really didn't care about his work per se when I was talking to him. I was really interested in his life, his memories, and knowing what kind of shoes he wore, what brand of cigarettes he smoked in 1939, what kind of music he listened to, and which bus line he rode. That's the kind of stuff I wanted to know. It really didn't have anything to do with, "How did you come up with the character of Sand Saref" or anything like that. I didn't have any questions about his work at all. It was much more like, "How did you know that a comic book was selling well? How long did it take you to find out if it was a flop? What were the sales receipts like?" That kind of stuff.

Murphy: That personal angle really shows through in *Kavalier & Clay*. You can see these characters are so three-dimensional that there were times reading the book that I forgot, with my steeped history in comic book geekdom, that I was reading a novel centered around fictional characters. Every once in a while I'd have to stop and go, "Oh, wait a minute." I got so incredibly lost in that book because it was a very, very rich world. It wasn't just about guys creating comic books.
Michael Chabon: Thank you. That's what I was striving for.

Murphy: I met Eisner a couple of times, and I imagine he would be amazing to sit down and try to get that information from.
Michael Chabon: He was very gracious.

Murphy: He saw all aspects of the comic industry, not just the artist or the writer but also as the editor and publisher. He was a comic book auteur. But going back to *Kavalier & Clay*. In your book, The Escapist, the fictional comic character created by Kavalier and Clay, was additionally depicted in other media forms popular in the 1940s, including serialized films and radio programs. In reality, The Escapist has been turned into a comic. With the way National Public Radio loves you, have you thought about an Escapist radio program?
Michael Chabon: No, I never have and it's not come up.

Ramirez: Were they to call you, would you work on something like that?
Michael Chabon: If I had time. Of course, why not, if somebody thought it was a good idea. I don't know how well escape artistry plays on the radio. It's kind of a visual thing, like, "Oh the chains, they're open."

Murphy: "Look at that guy down there?" "You mean the one with the key on his shirt?" "Yeah, that's him. He's all chained up!"
Michael Chabon: Exactly, you kind of want to see the effect.

Murphy: Well, radio in the 1940s and 50s was so infused in popular culture. You had the *The Adventures of Superman* radio program, and it seems very natural *The Escapist* would be in there. But when I have my high school students listen to radio programs, it's the first time they've ever been exposed to this medium. It's like, "What? They had stories on the radio?"
Michael Chabon: Oh, I know. It's still very effective. We have an XM Sirius radio in our car and XM has an old-time radio channel they play. I'll put it on for my kids, and it depends on what show it is. Some of them go over their heads, but if it's like *The Green Hornet* or *The Lone Ranger* or *Superman*, they just eat it up. They knew how to do it back then. My kids will get sucked right in and when it ends they go, "Is there another one?" I'll say no, because now comes *Dragnet*, and they're not into *Dragnet*. It's like, oh we want more. So it still works.

Murphy: So, if NPR called . . .
Ramirez: Which doesn't sound likely, but still . . .
Murphy: Who would you have play The Escapist? I'd say Campbell, Bruce Campbell.
Michael Chabon: Oh sure. He's got a good voice. You wouldn't be able to see his chin.

Murphy: Actually, his chin is so big it would probably manifest itself somehow.
Michael Chabon: You can hear people smiling.

Murphy: He's got a good voice. Kind of quirky, not quite so serious—that would play well with radio. Regarding *The Final Solution* and your literary knowledge of Sherlock Holmes in terms of style, how did you want to sound compared to Sir Arthur Conan Doyle, and how did you tailor your novel's voice to give it a Doyle feel but not overwhelm a modern audience with a Victorian-era narrative?

Michael Chabon: I definitely did not want to sound like Conan Doyle or the Victorian-era prose style in which Dr. Watson narrates the stories. I didn't want to write a pastiche like a *Seven-Per-Cent Solution* kind of thing. That's actually how I started out in this business, by writing a Sherlock Holmes pastiche when I was eleven or twelve years old. I did try to consciously imitate Conan Doyle and Dr. Watson's voice, and I was very much inspired to do so by the *Seven-Per-Cent Solution*, a great book that I loved. But with this one I wanted to write a very much more interior kind of narrative in which the characters are almost approaching a stream of consciousness in some passages. So my model was Virginia Woolf—I didn't actually go to her work and look at it to consciously, even to deliberately imitate it. I just invoked it in memory, the experience of reading certain Virginia Woolf novels, the ones where you have a combination of diction that is still clearly coming out of a late Victorian-Edwardian way of speaking or writing. So, I tried to write both that visual sensory intensity you find in Virginia Woolf along with diction that feels British, feels Edwardian, but also has a distinctly modernist quality to it. That was much more the effect I was going for.

Ramirez: As a follow-up on that, what was the effect you were going for in *Gentlemen of the Road*, because there you had the tenth-century Caucasus thing going?

Michael Chabon: I wanted a sense of strangeness. Everything was different then. There's nothing, in terms of technology, for example. There is no continuity between that time and this time. I was certain the way people thought and felt and looked at the world had to be different than it is now because of their contacts and their environment and their expectations and their sense of the world—everything was so different. Of course, there are going to be constants of human nature and behavior that would be the same. But I wanted to have a defamiliarizing effect because we are in a totally unfamiliar time and totally unfamiliar places. I wanted some of that to be reflected in the sentences, so I used unfamiliar words and images, and also sentences that are long and dense and remind you that you are not in Ogden, Utah, in 2009, that you are in the Caucasus Mountains. I wanted that sense of, "you are not where you think you are." I also wanted there to be a kind of rolling, rollicking—you know—horses and elephants charging. I wanted some of that sense of forward motion of attack and swordplay and sweep and things that go into telling a story like this about adventure on horseback. I wanted that to be reflected in the sentences, too. The length of the sentences is also in part the attempt to convey a sort of sense of galloping, of forward motion.

Ramirez: The humor I found was contemporaneous to a degree—the jokes. That's not something that's going to translate over centuries. So for the banter, it had to be more familiar?

Michael Chabon: I didn't have any sources I could go back to that far in terms of novels, but I definitely thought of Don Quixote and those guys. *Don Quixote* has plenty of gags, plenty of very modern seeming comedy, comedic interchanges. When you're reading *Don Quixote*, you have a sense that this is not our world. Things were different then. People thought it was hilarious when they got beat almost to death. Like that was funny.

Ramirez: Some people think that's funny today.

Michael Chabon: I didn't want it to feel like Danny Glover and Mel Gibson.

Murphy: Or Bob Hope and Bing Crosby.

Michael Chabon: Yeah. I wanted there to be a somewhat timeless sense of their friendship, of their partnership, that their humor with each other is very rooted in each of them knowing the other one's failings. The things they say to each other are always coming out of this simultaneous forgiveness of and irritation with the other one's shortcomings. I felt that's probably a constant in human interaction with someone you are best friends with. There's always this teasing. I feel like teasing must be a constant. I felt safe making that bet. Fundamentally, they have a teasing relationship. No matter what they might say about the other one or how irritated or frustrated or disgusted they might get, fundamentally they have nothing but respect and admiration for the other. That's also underneath whatever they are saying.

Ramirez: That definitely came across. Thank you so much for your time— we very much appreciate it.

Michael Chabon

John Joseph Adams and David Barr Kirtley / 2012

From *The Geek's Guide to the Galaxy* podcast. Episode 55. 29 February 2012. www.geeks
guideshow.com. Reprinted by permission.

Geek's Guide to the Galaxy: How did you first encounter the John Carter books, and what sort of an impact did they have on you?

Michael Chabon: I first encountered them in Page One Books in Columbia, Maryland, in about 1973, I guess, whenever Ballantine Books reissued them with those stunning Gino D'Achille covers. They appeared somewhat magically, like the monolith in *2001*, in a cardboard display dump in the bookstore, this beautiful display with a big piece of artwork on the top of it, and then I guess maybe all fifteen books in this display, each with this stunning cover, and it had a sense of obvious cultural importance, at least to me at age ten or eleven. It inspired this immediate desire in me to know more, to visit, to go there and see what this was about. What was this thing, who was John Carter, and what was going on with these green guys and red-skinned beautiful princesses, and flying boats and everything I was seeing on the covers of these books? And I bought the first one, and I loved it, and I went back and bought the next one, and then I discovered that the Science Fiction Book Club was publishing them with equally arresting covers by Frank Frazetta, in double editions, two books in one. So I started to get those, because I was a member of the Science Fiction Book Club, and then not long after that Marvel Comics, of which I was also a great devotee, started doing a comic book version of the same character, and that just kind of cemented it all in my mind. So I was having a multimedia experience with the character of John Carter and the world of Barsoom, and I branched out pretty quickly into the Tarzan books and *Pellucidar*, everything Burroughs wrote. Edgar Rice Burroughs was one of my first fan crushes as a writer. He was one of my first favorite writers, and I read a biography of him that was published around then that my public library had, this giant hardcover biography of Edgar Rice Burroughs, and I used to sign my name "Mike Burroughs Chabon." I was obsessed.

I did read my children *A Princess of Mars* when they were younger. I had kept in touch with those books, I had re-acquired the Marvel comic book versions of them, and then in the mid-'90s I wrote an original screenplay called *The Martian Agent* that was kind of a steampunk thing, before the term steampunk was really in wide circulation, and I drew very heavily on my memories of Barsoom and of reading those books in creating the Mars in that screenplay, which also had canals, and savage tribesmen, and weird creatures, and all of that. So I never lost touch with that material. It always remained very important to me, and it was in part because of my experience writing that screenplay that I ended up coming onto the radar screen of Andrew Stanton.

Geek's Guide: Based on the trailer, it looks like some changes have been made to the story. How did you balance staying true to the source material versus the needs of the current project?

Chabon: Andrew Stanton and Mark Andrews, his collaborator, had already made a lot of the hard decisions about what to keep and what to let go. They had already analyzed the multiple characters . . . say, there are three evil Thark chieftains, and we really only need one evil Thark chieftain, we don't need three. As you guys know, Burroughs introduces the idea of telepathy—everyone on Barsoom is telepathic. It's a terrible idea, and Burroughs realizes that very quickly, and completely abandons it eventually, because it makes storytelling impossible. If everybody can read everyone else's mind, you can't have secret plans, you can't have hidden agendas, and those are the meat and potatoes of storytelling. So even Edgar Rice Burroughs betrayed his own story, so in a sense we had his imprimatur. Another example is the fact that John Carter is immortal when we first meet him in the first book. It's a really bizarre element that Burroughs apparently derived from a popular novel of the time, and it has nothing to do with anything, it's completely irrelevant, and he doesn't even abandon it—it just withers away and never returns. As I said, they had already made a lot of those choices; they had already made a lot of those decisions. They had also made I think the very key decision to take material from the first three novels, and to sort of consider those first three novels in the series as a whole, and then to look at the entire matter of those three novels as potentially the matter for three films. Each of those films would be conceived independently to tell its own discrete story separate from the others, so that if you didn't see the first film and you only saw the second one you wouldn't be lost, you would be able to follow what was going on, and it would present you with a satisfying experience on its own. So there are elements in the first film, the one that we're talking about today, that don't actually appear in the novels until the second book.

And I think again, with all due respect to Edgar Rice Burroughs, who as I've already said is one of my great literary gods going back to the age of eleven, but he was making it up as he went along. He was writing by the seat of his pants, he was writing for money, he was writing very quickly, he was being paid half a cent a word. *A Princess of Mars* was the first thing he ever wrote, ever. He didn't really know what he was doing yet, as none of us would, as none of us did when we wrote the first thing that we ever wrote. And clearly he was remarkably gifted, that he was able to do such a good job on the first time out, but he got better. By the time you get to the fifth book, *The Chessmen of Mars*, that's actually a really good book, written by an experienced professional writer with a lot of words under his belt. Like any pulp writer of his time, there wasn't time to go back and ask yourself, "Does it really make sense for all of my characters' names to begin either with an 'S' or a 'Th'?" No, it's a terrible idea, it's really confusing. It was confusing to me as a kid. I had a hard time distinguishing Sarkoja and Sola and Tars Tarkas and Tardos Mors and Tharks, and Therns, and thoats. I think if Burroughs had had a little more time, or he had an editor who felt he had a little more time, they probably would have gone over those things and straightened it out a little bit, and clarified it. We were saddled to a certain degree with things that could not be changed, like the names of the most important characters, for example, but boy did we wish we could change them. Your ultimate goal is to create a good movie, or even a great movie. Your ultimate goal is not to literally transcribe the action of the book onto film, which would ultimately I think be doing a dishonor to the book, because you would be able to capture none of the rich, strange magic of that book in so doing. And therefore you're ultimately betraying the book.

Geek's Guide: I thought it was really interesting that in your memoir, *Manhood for Amateurs*, John Carter actually comes up during a conversation about whether or not to circumcise your son. Could you talk about that?
Chabon: [*Laughs*] Well, it was in the context of discussing with my wife the argument that many opponents of circumcision put forward that having a foreskin increases a man's sexual pleasure. You know, it's a tantalizing argument for a circumcised man to contemplate, but then it also involves a

certain amount of impossibility, of failure of imagination, because for one thing, how much more pleasurable do I need sex to be? It's already pretty awesome! And furthermore, what would that be? I can't even begin to imagine it, and in trying to imagine the unimaginable, whenever I'm confronted with a problem of, you know, irrational numbers, or string theory, anything that's asking you to imagine the unimaginable—greater sexual pleasure, in this case—I always come back to the nine colors of the Barsoomian spectrum. As a kid I just would try to imagine what other colors there could be besides the seven basic colors, and what they would look like, and how you would even know that's what they were if you had earthly eyes, and so on. And so that's how Barsoom worked its way into that particular discussion.

Geek's Guide: You've said that you started out wanting to be a fantasy and science fiction writer. How did you end up writing books like *Wonder Boys* instead?

Chabon: Well, it's not that I wanted to be a fantasy and science fiction writer, it's that I wanted to be a writer, and when I imagined the kinds of books that I wanted to write, they were the kind of books that I loved to read. So at any given moment in my life, from the point that I decided to be a writer forward, which was around this time—I discovered Burroughs and then Arthur Conan Doyle right around the same time, and those were kind of my first two crushes—I would imagine writing books that I loved to read. When I was in my early to mid-teens, that was a very heavy diet of science fiction and fantasy, so those were the kinds of books I tended to imagine writing someday, or even began to try to write. And just as I got older and read more, and read more widely, those imagined books changed along with my readerly diet, although I never stopped reading, and I still to this day have never stopped reading, fantasy and science fiction. I just started rereading Mervyn Peake's *Gormenghast* trilogy, which I haven't read in about thirty years, and I'm a big Iain Banks fan. I never abandoned genre fiction as a reader at all. After *The Mysteries of Pittsburgh* and *Wonder Boys* and the short stories that I wrote at the beginning of my career as a published writer, I was eventually presented with this puzzle, which was, "What happened to that idea of writing the kinds of books that you love to read?" And yes, the books that I was writing were modeled to some degree or another on other books that I loved, but my diet as a reader had never abandoned things that my output as a writer was just clearly not reflecting, and I wondered about that, like, "Why? Why does my backlist look so monochromatic, when the spectrum of my reading is so multicolored?"

And I didn't really have a good answer. I had a lot of shameful, cowardly answers for that question. I had been taught early on in college and graduate school that I wouldn't be taken seriously if I wrote genre fiction, and not only would I not be taken seriously, but people just really didn't want to read it, people like my workshop mates and my workshop leaders. I had workshop leaders who just out-and-out said, "Please do not turn science fiction in to this workshop." That was discouraging, obviously. If I had had more courage and more integrity, I might have stood up to it more than I did, but I wanted to be read, and I wanted to receive whatever benefits there were to be received from the people I was in workshop with, and the teachers I was studying from. I wasn't looking for a fight, and it wasn't like I don't love F. Scott Fitzgerald and John Cheever and Vladimir Nabokov and Eudora Welty and all those people. I love their work just as much, if not more in some cases, as Arthur C. Clarke, or Frank Herbert, or whoever it might have been. I had just sort of allowed myself to fall into this channel as a writer that at some point I realized I didn't want to be limited to anymore.

Geek's Guide: You also edited two anthologies from McSweeney's with the aim of exposing readers to a wider range of genres and making it okay for short stories to have a plot. How successful would you say that was, and why did the project stop after two books?

Chabon: I don't know. I would like to know how successful the project was. I mean, in terms of the short story . . . I don't think it worked. If you take a quick look at the—I'm always going to put this term in quotes—but at the so-called "literary" outlets for short fiction, I don't see a whole lot of ghost stories and sea stories and pirate tales being presented in the literary context. What I was really trying to do was rekindle my own interest in the short story form, which had abated quite a lot when I first began to contemplate what emerged as that first *McSweeney's* issue, number 10. I mean, I've written very little in the way of short fiction since then, so even on a personal level it didn't really work. But when you turn to the novel, you look at the most recent novels by Colson Whitehead, Gary Shteyngart, Rick Moody, Cormac McCarthy. There are so many examples. There's almost been a little floodlet of so-called "literary" writers either embracing or circling around clear literary genres.

Geek's Guide: Speaking of literary genres, you wrote this great Lovecraftian horror story called "The God of Dark Laughter." How did that story come about, and were you surprised to see it appear in the *New Yorker*?

Chabon: Well, that was actually sort of my second foray. I created this fictional character in the novel *Wonder Boys* of August Van Zorn, who we're told is a writer of Lovecraftian horror fiction who had an early influence on the main character of that book, and at some point I just got the idea to try to write an August Van Zorn story. You know, the pseudonym has always existed as a way to protect the "serious literary writer" from the taint of genre fiction, and that's how August Van Zorn used it. In the book his real name is Albert Vetch, and he writes under the name of August Van Zorn because he's a professor of literature and he has to use a pseudonym for that kind of sordid fare that he's cranking out. And that pseudonym was there for me as a kind of fig leaf too, to just imagine writing a straight piece of horror fiction that wasn't "meta" or, you know, sort of playing with the tropes of horror fiction in a literary way. I just wanted to write a straight-out story about awful goings-on in this small western Pennsylvania town that turned out to be rooted in some ancient cult of the Elder Ones, just straight-ahead Lovecraftian Mythos kind of stuff, and I guess I felt when I did that that I had to protect myself under that pseudonym of August Van Zorn that I had created—it was a double fiction at that point. And I wrote a story that was called "In the Black Mill." When I finished it, I thought it came out well. I believe my agent sent it to the *New Yorker*, who wouldn't even . . . it spent a very brief period of time on the editorial desk there before reemerging with its dignity somewhat in tatters, and then she sent it to a great fiction editor who used to be at *Playboy* named Alice Turner, who was a great champion of all kinds of genre writing in the literary context. She took it and wanted to publish it, but she insisted that I publish it under my own name. And god bless her, because that was right. I wrote that story, and if I want to write a piece of Lovecraftian horror fiction, I not only have the freedom to do so, but I also ought to be proud of it, and put my name on it, and let it just go out there along with everything else that I've written. So that was published in *Playboy*, and it got a little bit of attention from the horror fiction crowd, and it got included in *The Year's Best Fantasy and Horror*, and that encouraged me.

And so at some point a little idea popped into my head about clowns, and what if clowns really looked that way, and it wasn't make-up at all. There's something really horrifying to me in that thought. I mean, "coulrophobia" has a name because a lot of people think clowns are terrifying and creepy, it's not just John Wayne Gacy's fault. There's something about a clown in the abstract, with the white skin and the red mouth and all that. It's bizarre anybody could have ever thought it was anything but horrifying, in my opinion. But in any case, just trying to get at that, and wonder about clowns, and why they look the way they do, and in trying to answer that question, the answer occurred to me in the form of a horror story. This time I just wrote it without any monkey business about it being by August Van Zorn or any of that, but I set it in the same fictional Van Zornian universe of Plunkettsburg, which is the western Pennsylvania town that he set all his fiction in, as we're told in *Wonder Boys*. That was more for my own pleasure then, it had nothing to do with wanting to wear a fig leaf of respectability anymore. Maybe it's proof that something had changed, because my agent sent that one first to the *New Yorker*, and they took it, and maybe part of the reason for that is because it was a little more thinkable, a little less unacceptable, for them to publish a piece of straight genre fiction, and the fact that they've published Stephen King since then suggests that there has been a change.

And that's as it should be, because that's where it all comes from. One of the points I was trying to make in those McSweeney's anthologies, and in the introductions I wrote for those, is that it was not even 100 years ago—and certainly as long ago as 150 years ago—when all kinds of incredibly important work was being done by writers in France, and England, and Russia, and Germany. The great European literary nineteenth-century tradition is a genre tradition, and it's unmistakably, unashamedly, unabashedly in the works of the greatest writers of the nineteenth century. You find sea stories and ghost stories and adventure stories and early forms of proto-science fiction and fantasy across the board. And that kind of boundarylessness, or literary realms where the boundaries are very porous and indistinct and can be reconfigured at will, is much more interesting and appealing to me as a writer than a world where the categories are really set and really distinct, and the boundaries are really high and people have to stay where they start, and can't move out of those categories. That's just inherently deathly. And the reasons why it changed are bad reasons. They're economic and financial and marketing kinds of reasons, and they have to do with snobbery and academic laziness. There are almost no good reasons involved for that change that took place since writers like Dickens, who wrote crime fiction and supernatural fiction as easily as social realist fiction, and often all in the same story.

Geek's Guide: You also just had a short story in the *New Yorker* called "Citizen Conn." Could you say what made you want to go back to the theme of comic book creators?

Chabon: That was actually a story I had started a while ago and had abandoned because I couldn't figure out how to finish it. I stumbled across it and reread it, and suddenly it was clear to me how it needed to be resolved, and I rewrote it. In a way I returned very literally to a fictional world I had left behind, because I started that story a while after [*The Amazing Adventures of*] *Kavalier & Clay*, but not so long after. I think some stories just take that long. That one took a decade to write, and I've had that experience before with returning to a short story that I wasn't able to finish, and after many years suddenly having it become clear to me what needs to be done. I think it's just part of the process sometimes. But it wasn't like I made any kind of deliberate decision of "Oh, now it's time to go back to comics" at all. I truly just was going through my hard drive looking for something, and I saw that file, and I opened it up, and I was like, "Oh my god, I forgot about this story. Wow, this is actually kind of a good beginning, why did I stop working on this?" And then I got to the point where I had left off and thought, "Oh, I remember now. I couldn't figure out what to do. Now what about this?" It was just an accident.

Geek's Guide: Finally, are there any other new or upcoming projects that you'd like to mention?
Chabon: Well, I have a novel coming out in September from HarperCollins called *Telegraph Avenue*. That's the main thing, the only for-certain thing. I'm working on a project at Disney right now, a film called *Magic Kingdom*. I'm doing a revision of a preexisting script, working with Jon Favreau, but that's still in the pretty early stages. And then my wife and I are developing a TV series for HBO with strong genre connections, which is called *Hobgoblin*, and it's about a team of con artists and stage magicians and various charlatans who are assembled by British intelligence during World War II to fight against German spies. We're having a lot of fun with that one, but that's also a long way away from any kind of certainty.

Michael Chabon's Vinyl Draft

Michael Mechanic / 2012

From *Mother Jones* September/October 2012. Web. Reprinted by permission. This interview has been reprinted in full as a courtesy of *Mother Jones* magazine.

Craving Ethiopian, the novelist Michael Chabon—plaid shirt and jeans, man purse made from upcycled inner tubes, signature locks cropped to where he might pass for some mere literary mortal and not the author of a half-dozen bestsellers—strolls up a sidewalk not far from the Oakland-Berkeley border, where he lives with his wife, author Ayelet Waldman, and their four kids. This scruffy stretch is the setting of Chabon's new book, *Telegraph Avenue*, a Tarantinoesque romp following the struggles of two families, one black, one white, as a megastore threatens the husbands' vintage-vinyl shop, Brokeland Records, and a clash with an arrogant doctor lands the wives' midwifery practice in jeopardy.

Chabon was only twenty-four when he published his first hit novel, *The Mysteries of Pittsburgh*, followed some years later by a second bestseller, *Wonder Boys*, which was later made into a movie starring Michael Douglas and Tobey Maguire. Over the next fifteen years or so, Chabon cemented his rep as a genre-busting—mystery, sci-fi, young adult, comics—master of language and crafter of metaphor, winning a Pulitzer Prize for *The Amazing Adventures of Kavalier & Clay* and creating an alternate Jewish homeland in Alaska for his fabulously unique novel, *The Yiddish Policemen's Union*. His swashbuckling *Gentlemen of the Road* (working title: *Jews with Swords*) is set in tenth-century Khazaria while *Summerland*, intended for younger readers, sends us leaping among baseball-obsessed parallel worlds under threat from a dark character called Coyote. Back in Oakland, between mouthfuls of *doro wat*, the author tells me of his presumed kinship with Harriet Tubman, his "big internet problem," and why he considers himself a failure. No, really.

Mother Jones: Your last few novels were set in these fantastical worlds. What compelled you to bring it back home, so to speak?

Michael Chabon: It really all started with the record store. I grew up in Columbia, Maryland, a planned community built during the sixties. During the early years it was very integrated. I grew up being taught by black teachers with black principals and vice principals and, you know, a lot of black friends. We played in mixed groups, and I kind of thought that was how it was. Much later in life I realized that I had completely lost that. I was living in an all-white neighborhood in Los Angeles when the O. J. Simpson verdict came down and the primary thing I felt was, "How did I not know that's how black people were going to respond?" I had come so far from the kid who thought that, you know, Harriet Tubman was my forebear, to living in an isolated cocoon. That was a stark, painful experience for me.

One day a couple of years later, I walked into Berigan's, an Oakland record store that's not there anymore. There were two guys working there— one black guy and one white guy. The customers were a mixed-race group, different ages, and they were all just hanging out, shooting the shit. It just really resonated for me, seeing that little pocket where people had somehow managed to create—in this limited context, granted—a world that reminded me of the world I grew up in. It was very powerful. That made me feel like I wanted to write something that would be set in Brokeland, that kind of ragged overlapping border between Berkeley and Oakland.

MJ: Your main characters really struggle to embrace diversity.

MC: 'Cause it's really hard to do! [*Laughs.*] It may not even really be possible, and they're all aware of that. But some things are globally impossible but locally possible. And I think that's kind of what the record store represents.

MJ: How did you do your research for this book? Did you just hang out down here?

MC: Yeah, walking out the door: That was research. That was probably the single biggest difference for me in writing this book and writing its predecessors. From *Kavalier & Clay* forward through *The Yiddish Policemen's Union*, I had to check everything. Like, if you lived in a boarding house in 1941 in New York City, where was the phone? Was it downstairs in the hallway? Would you have to knock on your landlady's door to use hers? Or in *Yiddish Policemen's Union*, well, are they using US postage stamps or do they have special territorial postage stamps? *Gentlemen of the Road* was another example. To write a book where I didn't need to do research just for the nuts and bolts of everyday life was a big relief.

MJ: It's pretty bold for a white author to write a novel with mostly black characters. Did you feel any trepidation?
MC: [*Pauses.*] Sure, yes. Because I wanted my characters to be plausible and credible, and so that was a source of anxiety. And then as a secondary source of anxiety: What are people going to think or say or make of this? Would, for example, a black reader be offended by seeing me go to the point of view of a black female character? I thought about it. I didn't really worry about it. The truth is, I really only worried about that kind of stuff when I wasn't writing.

MJ: Did you have any black friends read it?
MC: Yeah. And that was actually helpful. I feel like I did make some mistakes and I overdid certain things, I would say, in terms of dialogue.

MJ: There is a sort of Blaxploitation element, with the amped up metaphors and Tarantino references. Were you aiming for a Tarantino aesthetic?
MC: No. I'm a big fan of Tarantino's work, and I think I'm fascinated by his evident sense of entitlement to use black characters and black material that he feels not simply comfortable with, but that it's his right and privilege—the apparent ease with which he handles black characters, fully aware that he's been criticized for that, too. But I think that motif, that theme, that subject came into the book because I came to realize was how rooted in the 1970s my characters are, musically and biographically. That's the decade that shaped their consciousness of what it means to be a man, what it means to be black or white, what good music is, and that really seemed to jibe with the setting. So the Blaxploitation stuff just fell in naturally.

MJ: How did this story come about?
MC: This book had a really difficult birth or parturition, because I made a big mistake early on. This thing started out as a proposed series for TNT. I wrote a ninety-minute pilot called "Telegraph Avenue" that had the same characters: The two guys, Archy and Nat, own the record store. The two women, Aviva and Gwen, were nurse midwives together.

MJ: What happened?
MC: They didn't think it was right. It never got past the script stage. I put it aside. But I think partly because I was living in the world of that story

every day and because I really love the characters, I decided to go back to it. I mistakenly thought all I needed to do was novelize it. Well it turned out that was just idiotic. And I spent two years wrestling with that laziness. Because—it seems so obvious in hindsight—a TV pilot doesn't do anything that a novel does. A TV pilot is all about setting the table. It's opening doors and leaving them open, and they're the doors that you're gonna go through to tell stories in the course of the series. Oh, it was a horrible structure. You try to make a novel out of it! I spent two years trying to before finally deciding just to abandon the novel completely. My wife talked me out of it. She loved Archy; she loved Gwen especially. And she just said, "You can't do that! I need you to write this book." Anyway, I kept the same characters and settings but I just reconceived the whole thing.

MJ: You invent some pretty wild metaphors. Do they just pop into your head?

MC: I'm going to slow this process down, because this all takes place in a second at the most, but normally I have an intuitive sense that something, a visual or a process or whatever it may be, is *like* something else: This woman's haircut: I see it in my mind and then I think, "What is it like?" And then I'll think, "It's like a Volvo—it's like the back end of a Volvo from the 1970s." And then I'll think, "That's it!" That's just right, because I also want to imply that this woman is very cautious and safe, and very white, and very—all the things that come when you think of Volvo.

MJ: You're known also as a master of cool, obscure verbiage. How do you add new words to your repertoire?

MC: I have a good memory for words, and when I come upon a word I don't know, I remember it, or try to—it's almost like a tic. I also just have a good feeling for how words are made and formed in English and the etymologies that give you prefixes and suffixes. So sometimes I'll think, I wonder if there is a specific individual word for this three- or four-word phrase that I'm trying to come up with. And I'll think, if there were such a word, it might be a word like . . . whatever. And I'll base my guess on that knowledge of French and my knowledge of how roots are formed with suffixes and prefixes in English, and Latin elements. And I'll think, it might be a word like *blahblahblah*. And then I'll go look it up and a lot of times my guess was right.

MJ: One section of the book, which I like to call "The Flight of the Parrot," consists of a single twelve-page sentence!

MC: [*Laughs.*] I couldn't stretch it any longer. That's where I ran out of steam. Otherwise I would have done sixteen. I wanted to have a chapter that would check in on all the characters—kind of a tracking shot like the opening of *Touch of Evil* or that famous tracking shot from *The Shining*—where I was swooping in and out of the characters at this moment in the story. Well, who could do that besides the author? And I thought, well, a parrot could do that if the parrot got loose. It just felt like the right way to approximate that was one single uncut sentence.

MJ: Who have you been reading lately that you're into?
MC: I'm back into Vladimir Nabokov for the eleventh time. I just reread *Pale Fire*—again. And then became completely obsessed with it, again, because I've been obsessed with it before. It's still probably the single most amazing book I've ever read. Now I'm reading *Speak, Memory*, Nabokov's memoir.

MJ: Anything more contemporary?
MC: The last new book I read—just completely burned through, adored—[was] *The Patrick Melrose Novels* by Edward St. Aubyn. It's a quintet about one character, tracing him from when he's five years old, and then you check in with him every ten to fifteen years or so. He just published the last in the series. It's fantastic.

MJ: In *Manhood for Amateurs* you wrote about starting a comic book club as a kid. And nobody joined, and that's when you started to feel like a failure. Do you really feel like a failure?
MC: Oh, yeah. Every single day. If nothing else, it's a habit.

MJ: In your work? I mean, as fathers we all feel that way.
MC: Right?! And that's something I contend with every single day. In my work, sure, absolutely. Nothing ever comes out the way I hope it will. That first vision, that initial vision you have of a book, what it's going to be like when it's done, it begins to go wrong the second you start to write.

MJ: C'mon. You must have had some experiences where a book came out better than you'd imagined—what, *never*?
MC: No. Because when I imagine it, it's perfect!

MJ: Unlike your sophomore novel, *Fountain City*, which you abandoned to start *Wonder Boys*. What was that period like?

MC: Long. Dark. Frustrating. Unfulfilling.

MJ: So was your early success a mixed blessing?
MC: I don't think that success was really the issue. I mean, it may have somewhat increased the feeling that I wanted to do something bigger, better, and different than what I had already done. But I would have had that impulse anyway. Other than that, it was just purely aesthetic. The truth is, I think I just wasn't ready.

MJ: And you didn't tell anyone you'd abandoned *Fountain City* for *Wonder Boys*.
MC: I kept it a secret. And, thank God, this other book just flowed so easily. I hit on the voice of Grady Tripp, the narrator, instantaneously, magically. I was like, I'm gonna try something different. I opened a file on my computer, started typing, and the words came out: "The first real writer I ever knew was a man who did all of his work under the name of August Van Zorn." It just came out like that. I didn't know who was talking yet or anything, but I trusted that voice. I don't know where it came from. I just followed it. I wrote a first draft of the book in seven months. It was completed in a year and a half, and that was very restorative, salutary experience.

MJ: So I gather you were one of those rare kids who actually knew what you were going to do when you grew up.
MC: I was very lucky. I had parents who loved to read fiction, who talked about it at the dinner table. I learned how to read at the age of four and immediately took with it, and was constantly reading. At a certain point I just had that fan-fiction impulse: You get so much pleasure from the primary work that you want to create a secondary work of your own to have it keep going. When I was in sixth grade, my English teacher assigned us to write a short story. I was in the throes of a deep infatuation with Sherlock Holmes and Arthur Conan Doyle and *The Seven-Per-Cent Solution* by Nicholas Meyer, which is a really great pastiche of Sherlock Holmes. And that really kind of gave me the clue that, wait, I could make my own Sherlock Holmes stories? How cool would that be? And I loved doing it. I loved imitating the voice of Doctor Watson and telling the details right. And I got an A and my parents gave me praise and that was it. I knew what I wanted to do.

MJ: You've described yourself as a solitary kid, and you chose a solitary profession. What possessed you to have four children?

MC: [*Laughs*] Well, when I'm writing, solitude feels very good, but when I'm not writing it feels lonely. And then, I'm kind of shy and not super social naturally—that's a learned behavior. Having a big family solves that problem. For my wife and I, it's going to be a good twenty-seven years of having people in the house, so I'll never have to worry about feeling lonely. I always have a whole crew around and they're into cool things and doing cool stuff and they like watching the same kind of movies and read the same kinds of books. We have our own little fan club going. My family ended up sort of taking the role I was unable to fulfill when I tried to create the Columbia Comic Club.

MJ: How do two bestselling authors, and prolific ones at that, manage a quartet?
MC: Well, that's why school was invented—to give your parents some peace and quiet during the day. I'm mostly working at night and so it's nice and quiet.

MJ: And you're nice and groggy in the morning.
MC: Exactly! I don't get up, usually. I get up two mornings a week, early, to be with them, and sleep in the other five.

MJ: And then you go off on little writing benders.
MC: Yeah. Routinely. I'll rent a place, borrow a place—my speaking agent has a little cottage that he loans me, up in Petaluma. I'll go anywhere I find that is quiet, has no internet. I have a big internet problem.

MJ: Do you wish all this technology would go away?
MC: Well, no. It's because I love the internet and it has been incredibly useful and I have made discoveries that have been immeasurably crucial to my work—things I don't know how I ever would have found out otherwise, that are perfect, just what I need for whatever I'm doing. And with that very truth is the pretext for all the bad stuff. Because I have gotten so much out of it that I can always justify or rationalize it to myself. I'll think, "Oh I'm just going to take three minutes to find out who made the spark plugs that were used in Mustang airplanes that they used during World War II." Two hours later, I'm, you know, looking at the Partridge Family fan site or something like that, and listening to "I Think I Love You."

MJ: [*Laughs*] It's called procrastination.

MC: It's more insidious, because you're being incited to it. Procrastination is something you do *yourself*. You know: "I gotta sharpen these pencils before I start. I got twenty pencils, they're looking kinda dull." Well, the pencils aren't calling you and alluring you and inviting you and offering you anything. They're just sitting there. *You're* the one who's procrastinating. The internet is actively trying to get you to stop working.

MJ: [*Laughs*] You mentioned a speaking agent. As this shy, socially awkward person, how do you feel about public speaking?
MC: That's different. That's a performance. That's easy. I have a hammy side of me that enjoys that.

MJ: Has anything else in your career come close to *Fountain City* in terms of disappointment?
MC: No, I've never had to abandon anything major and significant.

MJ: I guess this is the moment to ask about *John Carter*, whose script you helped revise.
MC: My disappointment was much more for the other people involved—in particular the director Andrew Stanton, who is so talented, so smart, was so conscientious. The narrative of the movie, its reception, and its fate was written before anyone had ever seen it. And a lot of the decisions the studio made about the movie were gravely mistaken. They never did anything to refute that narrative. The thing is, if you're going to like a movie that's set on Mars about giant green guys with four arms and red-skinned princesses and flying airships and barbarian tribal warfare, you're gonna love *John Carter*. If that just sounds silly to you, you're not gonna like *John Carter*.

MJ: Give me a quick Hollywood update: Is *Kavalier & Clay* ever gonna get made?
MC: I don't know. Right now nothing's happening. The movie got within a whisker of being put in production, but the plug was pulled on that in 2005.

MJ: What about *The Yiddish Policemen's Union*?
MC: Nothing. The Coen brothers wrote a draft of a script and then they seemed to move on. The rights have lapsed back to me.

MJ: Whom would you cast as your leads in those films, and also in *Telegraph Avenue*? You're God, so you can have anyone you like.

MC: As Sammy Clay, I would have John Garfield revived from the dead. And I always saw Adrien Brody as the perfect Joe Kavalier—now he's a little too old. I saw Rachel Weisz as Rosa Saks at one time, although Natalie Portman, who was gonna play her, is not a bad choice. For Meyer Landsman in *Yiddish Policemen's Union*, there's no doubt it's Elliott Gould, but at age thirty-five—Elliott Gould in *The Long Goodbye*. And this one? I haven't really thought about it. I can kind of imagine the guy who played Bunk Moreland on *The Wire*.

MJ: Wendell Pierce.
MC: Yeah, I can see him as Archy.

MJ: *Telegraph Avenue*—and your other writings, for that matter—are pretty nostalgic. How does nostalgia manifest itself in your personal life?
MC: For me, nostalgia is an involuntary emotion. There may be a song on the radio that I strongly associate with a particular moment in my history. And I can feel it for a time that I didn't actually experience, so, like, 1940s typography, or when a building comes down and you can see the painted ad on the side of the building next to it. I can remember feeling it when I was ten, not for things from my life but for things like those old soda machines with the glass door where you pull the bottles out, and you knew just from the look of them, they were an artifact of a lost era. I think it's just a natural human response to loss.

MJ: Do you collect things?
MC: Not religiously. I do have a collection of mid-century, small-press science fiction and fantasy hardcovers that is my most focused and dedicated collection. Everything else I tend more to acquire or amass than collect. I have vinyl records I listen to all the time when I work. But I don't collect records. I just buy records where the price seems right and it's music I actually listen to.

MJ: You and Ayelet recently sold HBO a pilot for *Hobgoblin*, a series about con men and magicians trying to undermine the Nazis during World War II.
MC: Yeah, they're perpetrating scams and cons. We're about to start writing the second episode. Once we've got two episodes, HBO will decide what to do.

MJ: And you've got a director.

MC: Darren Aronofsky.

MJ: You could play that idea any number of ways, from grim realism to sort of the Jewish answer to *Hogan's Heroes*. How are you leaning?

MC: Well, it's a drama, a World War II spy story, but because it has magic and con artists, there's a certain amount of almost bordering on whimsy. But it's life or death situations with people potentially facing death and the Blitz destroying London and, you know, the Nazis conquering Europe. It's not played for laughs.

MJ: You winced when I said *Hogan's Heroes*.

MC: [*Laughs*] I mean, I grew up on it. Everything I knew about World War II at a certain point came from watching *Hogan's Heroes*.

MJ: Except you're like, "Where are the Jews?"

MC: Exactly. I mean, what a bizarre—I completely took it for granted growing up, but now I think about it I'm like, wow—really weird idea for a situational comedy, these goofy Nazis. And yet, I remember it having real texture that was persuasive and convincing. It seemed like they got the uniforms right, and if you watched the show regularly you learned to recognize them: That's the army, that's the Waffen-SS, that's the Gestapo. I did get a sense of World War II initially from that show. But it was just a goofy '60s situational comedy set in a German Stalag.

MJ: Imagine pitching that today.

MC: I know! If it were today, it would be dark. Even if there were laughs, they would be dark laughs.

MJ: So, do you find working with Hollywood kind of infuriating?

MC: I've been lucky. I've worked with people I've really loved working with, like Andrew Stanton, Sam Raimi. I've worked with directors that I've really respected from their work and come to respect as collaborators. Jon Favreau, I worked with him, briefly. By and large it's been a surprisingly positive experience and it pays really well and you get health insurance!

MJ: I would think you could afford health insurance.

MC: Mm, we really depend on it. And there've been long stretches where we clung to that health insurance pretty tightly, where I took screenwriting work solely because the COBRA option was looming.

MJ: Critical acclaim and money aside, which of your books are you proudest of?

MC: The sweet spot, the soft spot of my heart will always be held by *Wonder Boys* because that was the one that saved me—that restored my faith in my ability to actually finish a fucking book. And it was fun to write after so many years of misery. And so I have this sense of eternal gratitude to that book. I'm very proud of *Telegraph Avenue*—right now, at least. It tends to fade in time. Then they just recede and they become Books You Wrote.

MJ: Do you ever feel competitive with other big-time writers, like, say, Jonathan Franzen and Jonathan Safran Foer?

MC: The only writer that I think I feel competitive with, but I mean it in the most admiring sense, is Jonathan Lethem. We're good friends. It's like what you heard about the Beatles and the Beach Boys, how when Brian Wilson heard *Rubber Soul* it led him to want to make *Pet Sounds*, and when the Beatles heard *Pet Sounds*, it led them to make—

MJ: You inspire one another.

MC: Yes, very much so. I don't think there was envy in that Beatles/Beach Boys relationship.

MJ: Really? As a musician, when I see someone great on stage, part of me is saying, "I wish I could do that."

MC: The writers that tend to give me that feeling are my betters, like Nabokov or Thomas Pynchon.

MJ: A female friend asks: Why does there seem to be this insistence that the Great American Novelist be male?

MC: I don't know. Maybe because only men would care about such a thing. I mean it seems much more a male activity to rate things in hierarchies. What a silly thing. Besides, it's *Moby-Dick*, so we're done. We were done a long time ago.

Chabon on Race, Sex, Obama: "I Never Wanted to Tell the Story of Two Guys in a Record Store"

Andrew O'Hehir / 2012

This article first appeared in *Salon.com*, at http://www.salon.com/2012/09/20/chabon_on_ race_sex_obama_i_never_wanted_to_tell_the_story_of_two_guys_in_a_record_store/ on 20 September 2012. An online version remains in the Salon archives. Reprinted with permission.

If you've ever lived in Berkeley, California, that much-ridiculed college town on the eastern shores of San Francisco Bay, or even visited the place, you probably have highly specific associations with Telegraph Avenue, a historic street of political protests and retail commerce (legal and otherwise) that dead-ends against the University of California campus at Sather Gate. Michael Chabon's new novel is pointedly *not* about that Telegraph Avenue, and its characters have no relationship to the university campus or to the 1960s explosion of left-wing activism that made Berkeley internationally famous—and, briefly, in my childhood, the locus of martial law as ordered by the governor of California, Ronald Reagan.

Chabon's *Telegraph Avenue* calls our attention, literally and figuratively, to the other end of the street, where Telegraph crosses the city line and becomes the main drag of the Temescal district, a racially and economically mixed neighborhood in northwest Oakland. That's where Archy Stallings, a thirty-six-year-old African American Gulf War vet who is the novel's central character, and his Jewish partner, Nat Jaffe (whose background resembles Chabon's own), are not so slowly running a vintage vinyl emporium called Brokeland Records into the ground. It's the summer of 2004, and a wealthy former NFL star and Oakland native, Gibson "G-Bad" Goode, is planning to open an immense new retail-entertainment complex—called, wonderfully, the "Dogpile Thang"—four blocks away, applying the coup de grace to Archy and Nat's failing business.

But if the Pulitzer-winning author of *The Amazing Adventures of Kavalier & Clay* and *The Yiddish Policemen's Union* started out with the aim of capturing one peculiar neighborhood's distinctive ambience, there's no mistaking the enormous social and cultural and literary ambition of *Telegraph Avenue* (which actually began life as a proposed TV series for producer Scott Rudin in the late '90s, before morphing into a novel). This is a book about the shifting nature of race relations in the twenty-first century, one in which a young senatorial candidate from Illinois who would, a few years hence, implausibly be elected president makes a surprise guest appearance. It's a book about the traumas and failures and transient joys of fatherhood in general—about which Chabon, who has four kids with his wife, novelist and essayist Ayelet Waldman, has always written wonderfully—and more specifically about black fatherhood, a topic few white writers would dare to go near.

Archy and Nat's ambiguous struggle against the Dogpile empire, and their far more important struggle to save their respective families, their friendship, and their shared dream, is nearly matched by the stories of their wives, who are business partners in their own venture. Gwen Shanks and Aviva Roth-Jaffe are professional nurse-midwives who've purged much of the herb-infused, New Age Berkeley-ness from their practice and established it as a legitimate medical resource, but who now face a many-leveled crisis after a home birth goes disastrously wrong. Throw in Nat and Aviva's teenage son, who is brilliant, eccentric, and probably or certainly gay; Archy's resurfaced teenage son, who Archy only dimly knew existed; and the deadbeat dad Archy knows entirely too much about—one-time Blaxploitation kung-fu star Luther Stallings—and a raftload of supporting characters, and you get a richly flavored, thoroughly engrossing stew of stories and ideas and themes.

Chabon is not a writer to let one metaphor suffice when two (or five) will do the job, but his style is so joyful and his dialogue so contagious that once I got in the swing of *Telegraph Avenue* I never minded the florid effusion of verbiage. Some of his character asides are so delicious they're worth the price of admission all on their own. At one point Archy reflects that in our age "everything good in life was either synthesized in transgenic cyborg vats or shade-grown in small batches by a Buddhist collective of blind ex-Carmelite Wiccans." Even better is Gwen's startling meditation on her deepening dislike for the Bay Area, "with its irresolute and timid weather, the tendency of its skies in any season to bleed gray, the way it had arranged its hills and vistas like a diva setting up chairs around her to ensure the admiration of visitors."

That's the kind of dislike that can only be fully understood by those who have lived in a place and loved it. When I met Chabon in the backyard of a restaurant in Brooklyn, New York, to talk about the opposite coast, I told him that I had grown up in Berkeley and Oakland, and once worked at a pizza parlor a few blocks from his fictional record store. (I left town long before he got there.) But those are irrelevant personal details that may restrict my enjoyment of the book as much as they augment it; he's clearly screwed if readers have to grasp all the geographical nuances or call up images of particular parks and intersections. I did not, however, tell him that an award-winning writer I know well completed a 1960s novel called *Telegraph Avenue* some years ago that made the rounds of New York publishers without finding a home. After all, somebody had to grab that title eventually, and Chabon's sprawling and thoroughly addictive book makes wonderful use of it.

Andrew O'Hehir: Talk to me about the title, because people who know the Bay Area, and even people who don't, may expect something very specific from a novel called *Telegraph Avenue*. And that isn't what you've given us at all.

Michael Chabon: I actually wrestled with that for a while. The title was always *Telegraph Avenue*, dating back to the time when this was going to be a TV series. As I was working on the novel and people would ask me what it was called, and I said "Telegraph Avenue," people either just got like, "Ughhh," or they would be like, "Oh! Blondie's Pizza!" And I would be like, no, no, no. Not *that* Telegraph Avenue. I started thinking of changing the title to *Brokeland*, and my editor talked me out of that. When I said *Brokeland*, people would be like, "Brooklyn? Brockland? What is it? Is it about the economy?" She really wanted me to go back to *Telegraph Avenue*, so I did. What's annoying now is that people keep calling it *Telegraph Hill*. [A prominent geographical feature of San Francisco, across the bay.]

O'Hehir: Well, that's just *profoundly ignorant*. You can't do anything about those people.

Chabon: Ultimately, look how many great books have terrible titles. I mean *Love in the Time of Cholera*, that's a terrible title.

O'Hehir: Is it? You remember it. Isn't that what you want?

Chabon: Because it's such a great book. But when he tried it out on people, they were probably like, "*Cholera*? You want to put that right in the title? It's a downer, man." [*Laughter.*]

O'Hehir: It's a lot about the way words sound, I guess. "Telegraph" is a great word, with a lot of cultural resonance.

Chabon: Yeah, and *Telegraph Avenue* scans really nicely too. It's double dactyls.

O'Hehir: These are the things writers think about.

Chabon: When they are supposed to be writing. [*Laughter.*]

O'Hehir: Let's talk about Brokeland, which is a lovely word, although I assume you didn't coin it—that border zone between Berkeley and Oakland, which is also a cultural collision between whiteness and blackness, and between lots of other things too. What was it about that area of the world that appealed to you so strongly?

Chabon: Well, I mean, it's where I live, essentially. We live in Elmwood [on the south side of Berkeley], so we spend a lot of our time down on Telegraph, between about 51st and 40th. We moved there in 1997, when Temescal [the neighborhood of northwest Oakland that adjoins Berkeley] was just barely starting to regain . . . It's one of those parts of Oakland that, like Rockridge [a more affluent adjacent neighborhood], was like almost killed by the construction of the Grove-Shafter freeway. Rockridge recovered a lot sooner, and Temescal was this historic neighborhood that was just starting to recover when we moved to the area.

I was just drawn to it right away. There was just something about that part of Oakland that was appealing to me. When I first started to think about this as a television show in the late '90s, almost on a hunch, I set the location of this fictitious record store on Telegraph Avenue. By the time I started writing the novel I knew the area very well, and I was convinced it had been a lucky guess that turned out to be right on the money. I did an interview just before going off on my book tour and I met the reporter at an Ethiopian restaurant on Telegraph [presumably the model for a restaurant in the novel]. Afterwards I crossed the street with a photographer, and right there on the corner I look in this half-open doorway, and there are vinyl records going down the wall and no markings on the outside because they hadn't opened yet. It was this used vinyl store that is opening on Telegraph Avenue right now, just blocks away from where I had imagined this book taking place.

O'Hehir: You know, I'm so cynical, especially when it comes to the Bay Area, that I would have said that wasn't possible now. But maybe it's more possible now than it was before the recession and the real estate crash.

Chabon: One of the things I enjoyed about setting the book in 2004 is that you have this dramatic irony. The reader and the writer know more than our characters, who are so terrified. We know that Dogpile [the retail empire owned by retired football star Gibson Goode] probably went under within a couple of years of this. A big tsunami is coming to flatten him, too. In a way, the cool thing about Berkeley and Oakland, and the little stores of Berkeley and Oakland, is that they hang on. If they die, something new comes on to take its place. People there will start a business out of passion, out of love. There are enough people who are a part of your church, whatever your church happens to be, to support you, at least for a little while, and you can sort of stand your ground. You know, Barnes & Noble came into downtown Berkeley and built a big store right across the street from Pegasus Books on Shattuck Avenue. Pegasus Books is still there, and Barnes & Noble is gone.

O'Hehir: OK, but what was it specifically about Berkeley and Oakland that grabbed you? Because this is a novel about a place that's also about race in America in the twenty-first century and about fatherhood and about a lot of other things. But before you could do that you had to get ahold of a story.

Chabon: Yeah, it was this one store I walked into. I've been engaged in this process, since I maybe turned forty, of reconnecting through my fiction, with parts of myself—my upbringing, my heritage, whatever it may be—that had great importance, that I had somehow lost or abandoned or forgotten or set aside. Comic books, in *The Amazing Adventures of Kavalier & Clay*. I began reconnecting to my Jewish heritage, especially with that book and then culminating with *Yiddish Policemen's Union*. Genre fiction, you know, just reconnecting as a reader.

And then the last remaining key element of my biography that I had wandered from, and in some ways the most painful to me—which took me a while to get around to facing—was black people, and their relative visibility or invisibility in my life, in sort of Ellisonian terms. I grew up in Columbia, Maryland, which during the ten or eleven years my family lived there tried and to a fair degree succeeded to be a very racially integrated, economically integrated, place where all were welcome.

O'Hehir: Yeah, I see where you gave a special acknowledgment to James Rouse, the planner of Columbia. That was a landmark in suburban planning, kind of the birthplace of "new urbanism" and one of the first, if not the first, intentionally integrated suburbs.

Chabon: Right. And in Columbia I grew up surrounded by black kids. They were in my classroom, they were my friends, they were my enemies, they were my persecutors and my saviors and my girlfriends and my teachers and my school principals, and when I left Columbia, I rapidly discovered that the rest of the world wasn't like that. It was a rude awakening for me.

O'Hehir: You've spoken a lot about moving to Pittsburgh and encountering a degree of white racism that you hadn't encountered before.

Chabon: Just startling. It would be like someone who was raised fundamentalist Christian encountering the raunchiest pornography for the first time. The most memorable encounter I remember was with a policeman, a Pittsburgh policeman, just hearing him so comfortably and casually spout the most atrocious kinds of things about black people who were nearby. And then this long period began, because of where I was living and what I was doing, where I drifted away from that experience of being around black people and living around black people—and feeling connected to African American culture just got away from me.

It was this day when I walked into this used record store, Berigan's Records on Claremont Avenue, that isn't there anymore. I saw the guys working there, a black guy and a white guy, and the customers were a mix and I just had this little feeling of like, here's a little tiny bubble that reminds me of that big bubble that I grew up living under, like a city under the sea. It just made me wonder: Why have black characters been so absent from my fiction, not to mention the circumstances of my life? I wanted to go there in fiction, but it is just another way of trying to reconnect to things that I see as having been a real source of strength for me in an earlier part of my life, and wondering if it can be that again.

O'Hehir: There's such a strong feeling of that in the book, and I can identify with that on a personal level. I think anyone who grew up in a multiracial context in the '70s and '80s will feel that vibe. I was also thinking about the history of race in American literature, which is such an enormous theme. I know this is the biggest cliché in the world, but in thinking about Archy and Nat and their record store, I was thinking about Huck and Jim on the raft.

Chabon: Me too. I mean, to me, Brokeland Records is the raft. You know, it's this magical space, where purely by volition on the part of the people who climb onto that raft all the hate and all the prejudice, and all the differences, kind of recede like the distant shores of the Mississippi on either side and you're alone in this state of mutual respect, affection, and shared interest. That's how that record store is for Nat and Archy, and I definitely, at some point, cottoned on to that aspect of it. It's very powerful, and I believe in it too. Even if it's a pipe dream I still believe in it.

It's what I heard Barack Obama, you know, when he gave that keynote address at the 2004 convention—what he was talking about, to me, was Columbia, Maryland. The America he was describing was the dream of Columbia, the vision of Columbia, I had grown up believing in. And it's a raft too. It's Huck and Jim's raft. It sometimes seems like a will-o'-the-wisp, but on the other hand it won't go away, as a beckoning image of possibility or potential.

O'Hehir: You have two white characters in the book who are really obsessed with black culture and involved with it. One of them is Nat, the record store proprietor, who refuses to "talk black" even though he grew up in a black neighborhood and had a black stepmother. And then there's his evil or comic doppelganger, Moby the lawyer, a Jewish guy who's always trying to be "down" and talk street, and is basically a figure of ridicule. Nat is obviously more like you—but how much did you have to contend with the voice in your head that was warning you about the dangers of being Moby?
Chabon: Oh, all the time, I mean always. And, I mean, just even growing up in Columbia—the word "wigger" had not yet been invented, but I was aware of kids like that. That was a style of being white, even when I was a kid in the '70s. And you can't make a generalization about it, I feel like some kids, some white kids, were able to do it and pass in that sense.

O'Hehir: There's always the model of Johnny Otis, the R&B legend who grew up in Berkeley, and who died a few months ago. People kind of forgot he was white after a while.
Chabon: Right, and there were other kids who were the object of ridicule, who could never quite pull it off, or you just sensed a sort of raised eyebrow in the way black kids were looking at that kid. It's not always doomed to failure, it's a strange alchemical thing. But, you know, I went into this project with my eyes open, and I didn't kid myself. I certainly didn't congratulate myself that my incredible powers and having grown up with a bunch of black kids somehow gave me the magical right to write from the point of

view of a black person. I just thought I could do it if I tried, and that's what I did.

But I was also aware the whole time that it's historically problematic for white artists to adopt modes of speech, or dress, or style, or music, or whatever it might be. There's this history of—you know, minstrelsy takes many forms. I wanted to always be conscious of that and be careful and be respectful, but also to signal, at least to the more alert reader, that I'm aware of this as a problem by using Blaxploitation movies, for example, as a key motif in the book. Blaxploitation was complicated, but sometimes involved white producers and filmmakers getting all the money, while selling these movies to black audiences. It's more complicated than that, but that was a way of signaling it. The character of Moby was a way of signaling it.

O'Hehir: Right. And it's not like Moby trying to speak in street idioms, and sometimes sounding foolish doing it, makes him a bad guy.
Chabon: No, he's not at all. It doesn't rankle any of the black characters as much as it rankles Nat, who is so studious about never "talking black." Whenever I find myself coming up against what feels like a stereotypical situation or character, my impulse is always to try to make it more ambiguous. Like, with the big-box store coming in to destroy the mom-and-pop business, the big-box store is really well intentioned and has a kind of progressive social agenda behind it, and is trying to bring jobs and self-esteem to this damaged neighborhood, and is owned by a black man. So with Moby, he is a figure of ridicule to a certain degree, but he's also a really sweet guy and he comes through in a pinch for Gwen when she's in trouble. Nothing's black and white, to coin a phrase.

O'Hehir: Maybe we can talk a little about the handling of gender and sex in the book. You've reached into two super-duper-male narrative modes, by going into the Blaxploitation movies and all the obscure record-store stuff, the jazz and funk and soul from the '70s. I don't think I'm off base in saying that the influence of Quentin Tarantino and Nick Hornby is hovering in the air over this book. You're trying to go into those ultra-male zones and make it out alive as a guy with some feminist credentials, and with a book that women will still want to read.
Chabon: Well, actually, now that you mention it—I'm a Tarantino fan. *Pulp Fiction* and *Jackie Brown* are two of my key movies, and I love *Kill Bill* too. But he's also a white artist who's been accused of appropriating black modes of speech and characters and using the N-word too freely. That was another

way of signaling that I know what I'm doing has a history, and it's not always a good history and here's another example of that ambiguity. You know, I never just wanted to tell the story of two guys in a record store. I always wanted, for my own interest as a writer, to find a way to balance it out. One of the more obvious ways to balance it out was by having some strong female characters. I'm on this never-ending quest in my writing to bring my female characters up to the level of importance and plausibility of the male characters. It's something I've been struggling with since the beginning, and I feel like with each book I've made progress in that regard. I feel like Gwen—she and Archy are the main characters in the book, and she may have marginally less time in terms of pages than Archy does, but I feel like I got fairly close.

O'Hehir: Well, and she and Aviva are midwives, which is arguably the most female-centric realm you could possibly have come up with!

Chabon: I began conceiving this idea right at the time when my wife and I were having a lot of kids. We were having our second kid and we used a nurse-midwife for that birth, and I got fascinated by that work. I mean, come on, it's like the most powerful job you can have, and I knew it would give juice to whatever work I put it in. I felt like we have this super-male world, if I want to balance it out, let's just go completely female on the other hand and have this stuff about birth and labor and see where it takes me and what it gets me. That was even before I started thinking of it in terms of race and the politics of hospitals and all that stuff.

O'Hehir: Was that the area where you had to do the most research?

Chabon: I knew a lot already, but I did research and I talked to midwives and it was really helpful. In terms of how much time I spent doing research, I spent a lot more time going to used record stores, buying records and coming home and playing them and listening to them and reading about music probably than I did researching the midwifery.

O'Hehir: How many guys, over the years, have used that pretext for buying old albums and watching old movies? And you're the one person in the history of the world who actually followed through. All of us have spent time assuring our wives and girlfriends that . . .

Chabon: "It's for work! It's a write-off!" [*Laughter.*] Part of what helps me decide which book to write is which one sounds like it's going to be the most fun to research. Like Yiddish, for example. When am I ever going to study Yiddish and read lots of Yiddish literature if I don't give myself this pretext? I have a self-improving streak, an auto-didactic streak, and part of the reason I like writing novels is because they give me the excuse to learn about things I didn't know about before.

O'Hehir: Archy and Nat seem to share the view that African American music starts to go downhill after 1990 or so. Are you going to get major push-back on that? That strikes me as a white-boy opinion.

Chabon: Oh, Archy doesn't feel that way, no. He won't subscribe to that theory. He likes hip-hop. I think Archy's heard it all before so Nat doesn't get a rise out of him anymore, but Archy's still keeping up with black music. He certainly would have made it all the way through the golden age of hip-hop, all the way through Tribe Called Quest and Wu-Tang. He's probably not that into Lil Wayne. [*Laughter.*]

O'Hehir: I always love the moments in movies or TV shows or novels where it feels like characters step into the foreground to have a conversation that is meta-textual or whatever, a conversation about what is happening in the work around them. But it really takes some balls to have Barack Obama be one of the people having that conversation. I understand that historically and chronologically, he fits. But how did you decide to put him in there?

Chabon: Well, there was the thematic resonance he had for me. I was talking before about that speech that he gave. It started out as a plot idea essentially or the solution to a problem I had. These guys are in a band and I want to show them playing together, I want to explore that side of their relationship. I needed to send them somewhere and I thought, well, they play in clubs. That's kind of boring. I could send them to a wedding and that sort of appealed to me. I knew I was going to have a funeral and I have a birth. Then I thought, nah, too much. So then I thought, well, political fundraiser and this is August 2004 so it's John Kerry. And I thought about a Kerry fundraiser that my wife and I went to in the Berkeley hills that year.

O'Hehir: Was Obama there?

Chabon: No, not at that one. But shortly after he was elected to the Senate, he did a fundraiser for somebody in the Bay Area, around the end of 2004. My wife Ayelet went to that, and she claims—I think with reason—that she was the first person to utter the words "Obama '08." They went to law school together, and she was kind of teasing him a little. He said, "Ayelet, be quiet," which she's used to hearing. But that memory bumped into the memory of the Kerry fundraiser and I thought, "What if it was Barack Obama?" and right away I was like: Yes, perfect. Because he would have just come from that DNC, just made that beautiful speech, the one that when I listened to it I thought about Columbia. This is the theme of the book, I'm writing about this whole thing. He belongs in this book.

You know, I think Obama's rise and his election mirrored the desire that I had been feeling for black people to be more visible in my life. And wow! My wish came true in such a huge way. There are two key days for me in the history of my own racism, my own blindness. One is the day the O. J. verdict was announced, when I was living in Los Angeles, and suddenly a million black people became visible to me. The primary thing I felt at that moment was, "Why am I so surprised? Why didn't I know that?" I should've known that this would be the reaction, that this would send people out to the streets celebrating and dancing, and I didn't. And the reason I didn't was because I haven't been paying any attention, because I've been cut off from this world, from these people, from this community that I used to be connected to.

And then the counterpart of that is the day after Barack Obama was elected president when, again, not just for me but for white people all over America, black people suddenly became visible. Everybody reported walking down the street the next day and just saying hi—black people, white people, greeting each other, smiling at each other, with this sense of "Here we all are, on this raft together, at least for one day." That moment fell within the period that I was working on this novel, and it felt like in writing this book I was contributing, perhaps. Certainly I was increasing the visibility of black people in my fiction, and maybe in the work of white writers generally. Everyone's kind of steered away from it, with the exception of George Pelecanos and Richard Price, and that's so much in a crime context. In bourgeois fiction, in family fiction, in novels that aren't about drug dealers, you're not going to find a lot of black people in the work of white people.

O'Hehir: Absolutely true. How did that happen?

Chabon: Well there's this painful experience I guess in the wake of *Confessions of Nat Turner* by William Styron, which kind of cleared the field in a way. It scorched the earth and sowed salt in the frozen ground. However valid the criticism [of that book] may be in terms of appropriation and colonialism and whatever ism you want to ascribe to it, I think it was an unfortunate thing if what it means is that generally speaking white people never write about black people. How can that be a good thing?

O'Hehir: You have many conversations between black people in this book. But having a private conversation in which Barack Obama is "talking black" with Gwen, at least a little, might be the riskiest thing in this entire book. I haven't seen this reaction, actually, but some readers of whatever race may not want to go there with you.

Chabon: Yeah, well, some people have complained that it's cringe-worthy or that it's awkward or that it was a mistake to do that. I think that's just completely wrong. I stand by my portrayal—not of Barack Obama the man, whom I don't know at all, none of us do—but of the public character known as Barack Obama. I've paid attention to the way he talks in many contexts: what kind of audience he happens to be addressing, small or large, white or black, whatever it might be. I paid close attention and I feel like I got it right. I feel like that is what he would say under those circumstances. And the other thing to say about his appearance in that scene is that he's still working; he's on the job. Even though he relaxes a little bit with Gwen and lets his guard down just a tiny bit, enough to talk with her with seeming comfort as a black person to another black person, what he says to her is kind of a platitude. It's like, "People who find work to do that they really love, those are the lucky ones." Duh! Everybody knows that. But it's the combination of his saying it to her at this moment, where this is exactly what she's wrestling with. A cliché or a platitude can be just as powerful as a profound insight if that's how you're prepared to hear it.

O'Hehir: Are you a fan of Obama's in general?

Chabon: Yeah, very much. I'm still incredibly impressed with him. When he completes his second term, then it will be time to begin to judge what kind of a president he's been. I've experienced disappointments, like so many other people who voted for him—and I did so much more than vote for him. In particular I'm disappointed with the drug policy and First Amendment stuff. But on the other hand, what my wife always says is that the reason we've worked so hard for him was so we would have the chance to be disappointed by him. Considering what he's had to deal with—not just this colossal disaster of the economy but this virulently hateful, disloyal opposition—he's done better than anybody else who could have become president could've done.

"A Realm of Mystery": An Interview with Michael Chabon

Brannon Costello / 2013–2014

Printed by permission. This interview was conducted by phone in two parts in December 2013 and May 2014.

Brannon Costello: I want to start by getting a little meta and ask you about the process of being interviewed. There are writers like Samuel Delany who are very insistent about treating the interview as a kind of literary genre, and on the other hand there are writers who are hostile to the idea of giving interviews. Of course, you've got a good example of a very familiar kind of bad interview in *Wonder Boys.* Over the years, have you developed a philosophy or an attitude toward the interview as a part of your job?

Michael Chabon: I think interviews are a little bit like restaurants. There are all different kinds, and there are all different levels both of cuisine and of service. Sometimes a lot of the interviews that you're obliged to conduct when you're on a book tour might be more on the food court model, where the questions tend to be pretty standard, if not standardized. A lot of times the interviewer may not have finished or even started the book that you're being asked about, so the questions get more and more flattened out and generic. But then every once in a while, even in that context, there's the mom and pop *taqueria* that does everything right, and an interviewer from a small, out of the way newspaper might hit you with a really great set of questions. Your set of expectations is like when you're a diner—I like to eat in small, strip mall restaurants too, and you sort of just change your expectations of what the experience is going to be like. In a way you can be more disappointed if a more in-depth, longer-form interview doesn't seem to go well than you are when you are just talking to somebody at the *Centerville Times-Picayune* and it doesn't go very well. I don't know if I've ever really thought of the interview itself as a genre, although as soon as you say it and paraphrase Delany I completely see that argument and I might even agree with it. But I guess I approach interviews ultimately the same way I approach writing books, which is as a reader first of all. I know how much I love reading interviews with writers, especially really good ones, really long in-depth ones like the *Paris Review* model. There are so many of those interviews that have been so important, riveting, informative. They even sometimes give you an entirely new perspective on not just the writer and his or her work but on your own work or on other people's books. I approach the idea of having to give interviews with that in mind and try at least to maintain some degree of that kind of enthusiasm. At the very least I figure, maybe even if I'm not enjoying it and it's not necessarily the most pleasurable experience in the world, at least maybe there's some reader who's going to enjoy reading it as much as I've enjoyed reading interviews with writers whose work I admire.

Costello: One of the advantages and challenges to being the editor of the book like this is that you get to do the last interview, so you get to pull together some of the threads of other interviews and follow up on some of their questions. The subject of genre is something that you and interviewers tend to return to, and I wanted to ask a couple of questions to extend some of those conversations. *Wonder Boys* starts with Grady Tripp's memory of August Van Zorn/Albert Vetch. In various ways he enables Tripp's career or draws him a pattern of what the writer's life is like, and I'm wondering if you could talk a little bit about the particular brand of pulp that you assign to Vetch. He doesn't write barbarian pulp, he doesn't write space opera, he doesn't write crime—his very particular genre is the weird tale or Lovecraftian horror story.

Chabon: You know, the first sentence of *Wonder Boys*, as published, was the first sentence that I wrote when I started writing that book—and it emerged in exactly the form that it has now. I have no idea, for example, where the name August Van Zorn came from. I think at first it just sounded like the name of a horror writer to me, and at that point in my reading life I had really left behind almost all of what would be termed genre fiction, with a few exceptions, in terms of writers I continued to read or would reread, which I guess is the way that I most clearly express whether I care about a writer or not. Those writers would probably have been Raymond Chandler, Elmore Leonard, and H. P. Lovecraft. I kept in touch with H. P. Lovecraft long after I had stopped reading his peers or reading writers working more or less in the same period in other genres that I might have been reading when I was younger. But Lovecraft had stuck around. I've always had a soft spot for him and his work, and I think that there was and there remains something incredibly appealing and important to me in the idea of what in Lovecraft's work is called the *mythos*, the shared fictional background of many of his stories, even stories that would otherwise appear to have nothing in common in terms of setting or characters. They still can be woven together into the same overarching fictional structure, and I think that aspect of his work kept me interested in him long after I had lost interest in a lot of other stuff from that same bucket, so that when I looked at that name, "August Van Zorn," and I thought, "that sounds like the name of a horror writer," then I just immediately made the leap to have him be a latter-day Lovecraft, someone writing Lovecraftian fiction more in the 1950s as the pulp market is dying.

And once I had figured all that out, which I figured out very quickly in the space of that first night, then that helped shape my understanding of the elements that were going to make up part of the story of *Wonder Boys*. For one thing, there's a strong western Pennsylvania setting, because I soon discovered that it was going to be set in Pittsburgh. And having this image of this writer who used western Pennsylvania in the way that Lovecraft used Rhode Island and Massachusetts somehow made me feel like the story was going to be more deeply rooted in place than might have otherwise have been the case. It also introduced the idea of haunting and someone being haunted by his misdeeds, and errors in judgment, and lapses and so on, in both his distant and recent past. As I got into this, I found myself working with this story about these sort of inescapable objects that keep following Grady Tripp, that he's trying to lose or get rid of but he can't. It's like there are things he has to somehow exorcise from his life, and I think that began to emerge for me from that initial starting point of having a pulp horror writer be present, but at the same time absent, in the narrative.

It started to click in other kinds of ways, now that I'm thinking about it: it gave me the pretext for Crabtree and Grady's coming together in the first place, because of their shared interest in August Van Zorn. It kind of establishes them as fanboys, of a sort, before the term existed, and that could be the basis of their friendship, since that kind of enthusiasm or passion is so frequently the basis for male friendships. It just started to pay all kinds of dividends for me almost instantly, which is why I kept it around. That tends to be how it works, very frequently, for me—there's an initial, impulsive inexplicable hunch or random . . . I hesitate to use the word *inspiration*, but some random *thing*, this bird flies into the window and you just grab it, before you really even know what it is, and then that turns out to be something that just keeps paying dividends throughout the course of the book—and if it doesn't then, at least ideally, you get rid of it, because it isn't doing everything that you need it to.

Costello: Keeping on this topic, a lot of your work both in fiction and screenwriting and so on has been a sort of conversation with early twentieth century pulp giants like Lovecraft and Robert Howard. The fantasies that those writers were conjuring obviously have a lot of sources and a lot of angles to consider, but there's also a lot of discussion, especially lately, about the way those fantasies are emerging from a particular sort of late nineteenth/early twentieth-century worldview that is inextricable from a particular view of race. My point here isn't to say that these authors are racist so we shouldn't read their work, but it's not that these were writers who also held some objectionable beliefs. In many cases those beliefs are really central to the sort of effects that they create, the sort of narratives they devise, and I'm wondering if you struggle with or have to think about how to negotiate that.

Chabon: You know, I don't waste a whole lot of time on that. The work has to be worth it, I suppose. I have to be able to derive a sufficient quantity of pleasure, broadly defined, from the work to be able to overlook, or even forgive, the lapses in judgment, or what appear to be lapses in judgment to a modern sensibility but would have appeared to be something very different at the time. Some work doesn't rise to that level, and you think, this is just gross, I'm going to stop reading this because it's offensive and it's not very much fun. But you know, I was just reading my kids *To Kill a Mockingbird*, which is an indisputably wonderful book from which all three of us are deriving incredible amounts of pleasure nightly. It's so beautifully written and full of insight, and compelling, and funny, and everything you could want from a book. I'm reading along, and I come to this passage where Scout and her brother are taken to the black church by their housekeeper, Calpurnia, and Scout's remembering and describing what the church is like, and there's a line that's something like "the wonderful smell of clean Negro in the church," and I came to that line just in time to stop and think—am I going to go ahead and read this line to my kids? And then we can have a discussion about what we again now perceive as Harper Lee's unfortunate lapse in judgment, or maybe even a kind of benevolent, benign racism? Or should I just skip over that line—it's like eight words—and just keep going, and we can keep enjoying the story? So that's what I did. Other times, reading other books, like reading *Huckleberry Finn* to them, for example, I sometimes made another decision. There, I did stop, and we did engage in the discussion about Huck's racial assumptions and Mark Twain's racial assumptions; but most of the time we're just reading for pleasure, and as long as we're getting pleasure—and again I do define that term pretty broadly—then it's better to enjoy the work and just forgive or at least try to understand the context.

That kind of stuff tends not to bother me when I'm reading Lovecraft. On the contrary, actually. Racism is human. The biases that enable a culture to feel superior, in some way, to a neighboring culture or to some other culture across the ocean, might be as ubiquitous, and eternal, and as wired into us as anything; and to try to put a *cordon sanitaire* around it, or censor it from our own minds and our library shelves in some way is absurd, it's misguided, it misses the point. When you're looking at a writer like Lovecraft—his horror, let's say, of brown people, of Jews, of immigrants generally speaking, whatever it might be—that kind of apparently visceral horror that he at least on occasion seems to have experienced as he was bizarrely attempting to live in Brooklyn for the brief period of his marriage to a Jew—you know, that obviously is still *horror*, and horror is what you to go Lovecraft *for*. And clearly that kind of thing was feeding what he was doing in his work to some degree or another, in the sense of these external forces that are always threatening to break through and overwhelm the kind of pristine New England Yankee reality of his various narrators. So without that we wouldn't have these incredibly gripping, amazing accounts of universal cosmic paranoia that have continued to please me for going on forty years now.

Costello: One way that you have had to think about this issue recently was the *John Carter* movie. I was wondering if you and your collaborators had to think about how to handle the Confederate hero-ness of John Carter. The different adaptations of John Carter over the years have played it in different ways—those Jesse Marsh comics in the '50s update it to World War I, but Marv Wolfman in the 1970s Marvel comics tends to highlight his Cavalier spirit. How did you think about how you wanted to figure his Confederateness and southern-ness and what you gain and lose by keeping the history that Burroughs originally gave him?

Chabon: Well, the truth is that most of those decisions had been before I came on board that project. Andrew Stanton and Mark Andrews, his collaborator, had already made those calls and had decided to keep him a Civil War veteran, had decided to keep him a Confederate, so they had already done their homework and read at least some of the critiques of Bur-

roughs and of the imperialist apologetics that those Mars stories, like the
Tarzan stories, are purported to represent. So they were already kind of
aware of all that and had made decisions to stick to the original story of
John Carter, but also to try to elide, or not to dwell a lot on, just exactly what
he did during the war, and to leave out what you find in the books, which is
that he owned slaves. They did definitely tone it down, but they didn't shun
it completely. I thought that was pretty sensible. It's supposed to be this big
action-adventure epic set on the planet Mars with flying boats and sword-
fighting and six-armed or four-armed green guys, so you don't want to get
all bogged down at the beginning with his field slaves and his house slaves
and all that. It's not what you're going for, it's not where you should start.

I actually think what you find frequently—and Burroughs is a good example of this—in contemporary criticism by enlightened contemporary
readers about the purported racism and imperialism of writers, especially
popular writers, of the past, is that it's mistaken, or it's oversimplified. Particularly when it comes to popular entertainment, we have a tendency to
oversimplify our predecessors and to imagine that we're far more sophisticated now than they were, which is of course just what *they* thought about
their predecessors. Now, Tarzan is a different thing, but when I read the
Mars books now, what I see is actually at times a surprisingly incisive cultural critic who is not necessarily glorifying imperialism or colonialism or
racialism at all, but is in fact criticizing it, exposing it in its absurdities. Burroughs in those Mars books is actually much more of a satirist than he's
given any credit for being—because he's actually not given any credit at all
for being a satirist! But that's really what he was. He routinely presents these
preposterous societies that are founded on some bizarre prejudice or bias of
some kind, and portrays very effectively the contortions that the people who
live under these thought-regimes have to go through in order to maintain
them. I actually came away from my deep immersion in Burroughs thinking
that he wasn't a racist at all.

But to go back, there is something I wanted to say about pulp writers,
how I think about them, why they're important to me. I've invoked their
shades in various ways whether by writing directly in the Lovecraftian mode
as I have in a couple of stories, or in the Robert E. Howard/Fritz Leiber mode
in *Gentlemen of the Road,* or in other ways, including handling the characters created by Edgar Rice Burroughs. What those writers represent most
strongly to me—writers like Burroughs, and Lovecraft, and maybe Howard,
ultimately, more than any other—is this image of the completely unfettered
imagination operating in an apparent vacuum of material or inspiration.

You have someone like Robert E. Howard living essentially his entire life in a hundred-square-mile patch of godforsaken Texas nothingness, growing up in this oil boomtown that went from one-horse central Texas town, to a teeming, sprawling, licentious, crowded, completely chaotic and rough oil boom town full of bad people trying to make money in various nefarious ways, to a kind of ghost town again, all within the space of his very brief life, and yet every night sitting down to his typewriter and just pounding out story after story after story set all across time in these fantastic kingdoms. His amazing power as a writer is that he truly seems to be seeing what he's describing, that you have this incredible sense that he's *been there*, when he's describing Atlantis or one of his fictitious kingdoms. That contrast between the apparent poverty of his surroundings—I don't just mean economic poverty but almost a kind of visual poverty as well—and the lush, lavish inventions of the imagination, coupled to that Herculean work ethic—these guys burned out their typewriters they wrote so much—that's how they become kind of totem figures for me. Edgar Allan Poe in his way is another example. He was more sophisticated and more traveled, and he did range from say Boston to South Carolina and up and down the Eastern seaboard at least, but he never went anywhere else. He certainly never went to the Europe that he described in so much of his work, and the preponderance of his work is again sort of lavish and baroque.

I'm just this guy sitting in a chair, you know? And generally speaking I haven't been to the places, haven't known the people that I'm writing about, and I try to work really hard to get my 1,000 words every day. So they're almost household gods to me, these writers, because even in extreme form, sometimes—and again maybe Howard is the most extreme form, not just for these reasons but because he did end his life so soon and so everything is more heightened and compressed—I find some kind of inspiration in their example, even though I do try to write more slowly and hence, I hope, better than they did.

The easiest thing to disparage about pulp writers is the poor quality of their prose, and Lovecraft certainly is guilty of writing terrible sentences, but Howard has incredible verve, just an amazing gift. I think these guys wrote so much and so quickly that any of us, even the most sterling prose stylist among us, would find his or her work suffered if he or she was trying to crank out ten- or fifteen-thousand-word stories twice a week for a penny and a half a word. The quality is going to suffer, and again I think Howard is a good example—if he'd felt like he could have taken more time he would have written better than he did, and he wrote well anyway.

Costello: That description of Howard and Lovecraft and the imagination is a good segue here, because I wanted to ask about couple of different passages from the essays in *Maps and Legends* that struck me while I was reading *Summerland.* In *Maps and Legends* you express an affection for the weirdness and strangeness of the Norse myths, and in another piece you express some regret that Philip Pullman in some ways betrays the vividness of his world or the roundness of his characters by making them serve a kind of narrowly philosophically motivated plot. It reminded me of a piece I read recently by Sean T. Collins that was about *The Neverending Story*, the openended weirdness of it, and how it contrasts with a strand that he sees in a lot of contemporary fantasy writing or fantasy fandom that valorizes the grand plan or the grand design. When you were writing *Summerland*, were you aware of a tension between the need to give the novel a shape but at the same time not leave out the openness of possibility?

Chabon: I'm generally speaking not a really great planner with any of my books—I very much adopt a seat of the pants approach to plotting and shaping stories. I'm not a great planner in any aspect of my life; it's hard for me to look ahead. At this point I've gotten out of the habit of doing it, so I almost don't know how. So it's partly that I just don't work that way, but also partly that so much of the pleasure of writing comes from the interplay that I started out talking about between the work and chance inspiration, the impulsive, inexplicable decision to say that, for example, a character has been employed as a lifeguard, and suddenly that aspect that you had no intention of including in your story, the whole craft and history of lifeguarding in early twentieth-century seashore resorts, becomes this huge element in your story, and you plunge into the research, and you make all these discoveries about that little-known pocket of American culture, and suddenly the whole novel is built on this aspect of seaside life in the 1920s that you didn't even know you were going to be writing about when you set out. When my work's going well, and even when it's not going so well, that happens all the time. And I feel like that's how my work is fed; but also that's the fun part of it for me, so that the less I plan ahead, the more opportunities for that kind of thing to arise there will be. Sometimes you have to work the other way, especially when you're doing screenwriting. There's a lot of insistence from the higher levels—and there are *many* levels higher than you are when you're a writer in Hollywood—on seeing the plan ahead of time. They want to see the outline, they want to see the treatment, they want to know what you're going to be doing and how you're going to be doing it before you do it, and that actually robs a lot of the pleasure for me. The fact that I have little or no room to make those kinds of chance discoveries does drain away a lot of the pleasure. On the other hand, it's incredibly inefficient to work that way. It's wasteful, and I often will spend even *years* working in what turn out to be blind alleys and end up having to get rid of everything that I've done because none of it is working. That's true in life too, and that's a consequence of being somebody who doesn't plan well—you find yourself a day late and a dollar short, or caught unawares by something that there's no reason why you should have been aware of it, except that you weren't thinking ahead. So there's a downside, there's a cost to it all, but in the end I guess I do the calculation and the pleasure of discovery comes out marginally ahead.

Costello: How far ahead of the publication of the chapters were you writing *Gentlemen of the Road*? Was it done before serialization started?
Chabon: Yeah, they very wisely insisted on that. So it wasn't truly serialized in the classic mode. It was a completed work that they then published a chapter at a time.

Costello: Well, all right. That ruins the fantasy . . .
Chabon: But I didn't have *much* time, and I will say that was definitely the closest I've ever come to the pulp writer experience. I only had about six weeks to write 35,000 words or 40,000 words or something like that. I had to work quickly and I did actually figure that one out ahead of time, and I plotted it out to a much greater degree than I normally do. I still left little uncertainties for myself. I didn't have to share the outline with them, so I didn't have to make it too detailed, and I did leave myself space on that outline where I wasn't quite sure how it was going to happen or how it would work, and then I figured it out when I got there.

I actually took that job in a kind of pulp-writer style, too, because my kids were in a school here in Oakland at the time, which had done this huge capital campaign. It's a private school, but not a very well-to-do private school, and they had managed to raise all this money so they could build a new library, a real library. The school didn't even *have* a library, it had a room full of books on the stairway landing. So it had constructed this library, and it was very beautiful, but when they finished they were out of money and they still had not bought any books. All they had were the old, tattered books, that were mostly donations in the first place, to put in this brand-new library. That seemed like a real shame to me, and I thought, "gosh, I wish I were John Grisham, I would just write a check and buy the books for the school library." And within a day or two of my having that wish, the

New York Times called up and asked me if I wanted to do this, and the sum that they offered to pay me was exactly the amount that it would cost to stock this library. So I don't know if I would have taken the job otherwise—it was just that this magic number appeared right after I wished for it, and I thought okay, I'll just do that and then donate the money and they'll be able to buy books for the library. And the end of that story is that then we took our kids out of that school the next year. We left it behind.

Costello: Thinking about *Gentlemen of the Road* and the pulp influences that we've been talking about, I was wondering how, out of that constellation of writers, you plucked Michael Moorcock for the dedication? Was there something about it that you thought was especially Moorcockian?

Chabon: I think it was just more that Mike is a friend of mine. I had met him a few years preceding the writing and publication of that book. We met through a bookstore in my neighborhood here called Dark Carnival. It's a science-fiction/fantasy/mystery bookstore, and it's right around the corner from my house. Moorcock had come to do some signings, and it seemed like every time he came I wasn't around. I had left some of my old books of his with the bookstore to get them signed, and somehow one thing led to another and we ended up meeting and getting to know each other. At the time, he and his wife were spending their summers here in the Bay Area, where it's much cooler than in Texas where they live. He was—he is—one of my favorite writers. He was such an important writer to me for a certain period of my teen years, with both his fantasy and his science fiction. It was such an amazing thing for me to get to talk to him, let alone have dinner with him or know that he had read and enjoyed *The Amazing Adventures of Kavalier & Clay* or whatever it might be. It was just such a fulfillment, in so many ways, for me, that when I sat down and started working on *Gentlemen of the Road*, I guess partly I was thinking that I would like to write something that would both do honor to him but also that he would hopefully enjoy reading, so he was sort of on my mind. And in some ways he—I don't know if it's right to say that he's the last, but he's *among* the last living practitioners of true sword-and-sorcery in the grand Leiber/Howard tradition, even though in his case he very much takes a kind of postmodern approach to it. The critique of the genre is built into the way that he wrote it, in a way that you wouldn't find in earlier writers. It's possible to read those Elric stories and the other stories in his cycle of heroic fantasy for the same pleasure that you would get out of Fafhrd and the Gray Mouser or the Conan stories—you don't *have* to read them as critiques, but I think Michael Moorcock would be happier if you did.

Costello: This ties in to thinking about *Gentlemen* in a very roundabout way, but one of the topics that came up a lot in interviews and reviews of *Telegraph Avenue* was the question of race. I don't want to revisit it in just those terms, but I did see in *Telegraph Avenue* the culmination of something that runs through a lot of your work about the nexus between Jewish culture and black culture, or maybe the imaginative use to which black and Jewish cultures put each other. It goes all the way back to "S Angel" in *A Model World*, where Ira is fascinated by the black saxophonist playing at the wedding; Joe and Sammy are investing Joe Louis with their hopes when he's taking on Max Schmeling in *Kavalier & Clay*; you have Landsman thinking of Robert Johnson as a "black Delta yid" in *Yiddish Policemen's Union*; you have Amram the Abysinnian Jew in *Gentlemen*; and there's a lot of detail in *Telegraph Avenue* about the figure of Nat's stepmother Opal, who speaks a "wild Negro Yiddish" and so on. So I was wondering if you could talk a little bit about what interests you about that connection?

Chabon: I suppose that's a connection that has very deep roots, not only, obviously, in American culture and society, but in my own personal history. Because of the depth and the foundational importance of that connection in my own personal history, the fact that I could see it echoed and reflected in so many ways, looking around me, from the time I became conscious of it as a child all the way through the rest of my life. It always attracted my intellectual attention and my intellectual interest, but also my emotional attention and my emotional interest. It's about becoming aware, at maybe around age five or six, that here we were, my family at the Passover Seder table, singing "Let My People Go"—which is a Negro spiritual, which I knew was a Negro spiritual—and here were these Jews sitting around the dinner table singing this song that had been composed by African American slaves a hundred, two-hundred years before, who were, in turn, conceiving of *themselves* in terms of *Jews* living in slavery in Egypt. The way the source became the seed became the fruit which in turn become the seed for another fruit, that kind of endless process of appropriation and adoption was almost miraculous to me, from a very early age—that it could just echo and re-echo. Maybe I didn't have quite this consciousness as a young kid, but I eventually came to have this consciousness that there was something peculiarly and wonderfully American about that, that only in this country could something like that have happened. For all of this sort of opprobrium that is attached to the term "appropriation," "cultural appropriation," black slaves conceiving of themselves in terms of Moses and the Israelites in Egypt is itself a form of cultural appropriation, and thank goodness! Right there, in that experience at the Seder table, is the sort of clear illustration of the hall of mirrors in which blacks and Jews have lived in American culture, where they're endlessly reflecting each other and being in turn reflected back again. You see that echoing down through the history of popular music all across the twentieth century, from one end to the other, from ragtime all the way up through hip hop, from Irving Berlin to the Beastie Boys and everything in between, including Leiber and Stoller and George Gershwin; and on the other side, all the black composers and musicians who drew, in all kinds of lesser-known ways, on the Jewish experience and on various Jewish forms of art and inspiration. Everywhere I have looked over the course of my subsequent life, I have found that fundamental mutual regard, and it's not something that I just sort of pay attention to; it's something that I *participate* in.

I grew up in Columbia, Maryland, in this deliberately racially integrated town in the Maryland suburbs between Baltimore and Washington, in a context in which it was not simply *possible* that I would choose black artists and black politicians and black leaders and black scientists and black inventors and so on as my heroes and sources of personal and creative inspiration, it was actually *expected* of me that I would do so. It was almost *demanded* of me. It was part of being a kid in Columbia in the early 1970s that you were not learning about Duke Ellington or Benjamin Banneker or Doctor Charles Drew from some sort of abstract obligation to recognize the accomplishments of black people for the sake of black people. You were expected to acknowledge the fact that they did the things they had done, not just for their fellow black people, but for everybody, including you. And I took that point of view and expanded upon it and looked around me and felt, growing up, that everything from the Jackson 5 to Muhammad Ali to Angela Davis and Roosevelt Greer, Rafer Johnson, whoever it might have been, all of those people were my people. Not that I wanted to be black, but that I was a white Jewish kid growing up in the suburbs and therefore those *were* my people. Because they were *everybody's* people. I had this sense of interpermeability of not just black culture and Jewish culture but of all the elements and strands that made up American culture at the time—it was all mine. Not just by privilege but by duty and obligation. I think that is ultimately what I was trying to reconnect with, in a more explicit way, in *Telegraph Avenue*, but as you say it's there all along. It's just not necessarily foregrounded.

Costello: One passage in *Telegraph Avenue* that makes me think about this is the moment where Gwen is not sure if Candygirl's catchphrase is something she said herself, or something a Jewish screenwriter came up with. The question of authenticity is set aside, it's not easily determinable; you can't trace what appropriation really is anymore.

Chabon: I recognize that the term "appropriation" means when a representative of a dominant culture takes elements from a subjugated, or in some way underprivileged culture, and that's why we're meant to disapprove of it. I do get that, but, especially in American culture, it's always going to be a futile effort to try to somehow put a stop to that. Because that's what we were, that's how we came to be, and it does flow in every direction, it flows up and down and laterally. You might feel like morally you need to think about the top-down kind of appropriation and say that's a bad thing, and maybe it is, but it's not going to do anything to stop it, because that's how it works here, and it always has. And again the African American reconfiguring of the flight from Egypt myth to suit their own purposes is a perfect example of that. You might call it Jewface, in a kind of analogy to blackface.

Costello: Thinking about those questions, then, of the sort of mixing and mashing and of American culture we see in *Telegraph Avenue*, I was struck by the cards that Luther is buying at the very beginning of the novel—before the era of home video or video on demand these were the only ways you had to extend the experience of a piece of art or culture that you really enjoyed, but they were so badly printed, so weird, and yet so evocative. I'm not necessarily asking you to wax nostalgic for those, although we can, but could you talk about the ways in which how we consume culture now has changed the way that you relate to it or changed how you think about the sorts of imaginative networks that get created when you're making culture in a time when everything is on demand?

Chabon: That's actually something I think about almost every day in some way or another, especially as the father of four kids, watching the ways that they connect to and relate to their contemporary popular culture, but also in attempting to educate and inform them about mine, and about the culture that preceded me, in my father's generation. My dad was born in 1938, but I think it's really from the early or mid-1930s, and the really widespread penetration of radio and movies, that you get the first sort of great era of popular culture, what I think of as true modern popular culture in America. It's so utterly different than it was when I was a kid, it's so much easier to get ahold of whatever it is you might want, whether it's simply information—discographies, filmographies, biographies—or whether it's actual artifacts themselves, on eBay or whatever. You can get everything you want, instantly, in a way that was just impossible, and was left so much more completely to chance, when I was a kid. The example that I like to give is the example of the Marx Brothers: that's me, trying to connect to the pop culture of my father's generation or the one a little bit before that. When I became aware of the Marx Brothers, it was because of a book that was called *Why a Duck?* that was on the shelf of my branch of the Howard County Public Library. It was like a collection of fotonovelas, photographs captioned with word balloons like comics, and it was essentially a scene-by-scene or shot-by-shot reconstruction of a half-dozen or so best-known Marx Brothers movies, with all the dialogue in balloons. That was all I could know about the Marx Brothers, because at that moment the movies were not showing in theaters, and they weren't being shown on television either, because there was some kind of complicated legal thing that was preventing them being shown. So all I could know about the Marx Brothers was whatever my father or other adults could tell me. There was an entry for Groucho Marx in the World Book Encyclopedia with his brothers' names as well, and then there was this book. And that was it. And I became a Marx Brothers fan based on that and that alone. And then a couple of years later, that legal thing got fixed, and the movies did start to be shown on television, and I watched them with great pleasure, and I have continued to watch them ever since. But you just took what you could get back then, and very frequently what you could get was not very much.

It's like everything else, and especially everything connected with the internet, it's almost a perfectly ambiguous situation. Or I should say I view it with perfect ambivalence, in that I myself, as a fan, avail myself every day of my ability to find out whatever it is that I want to know about whatever I'm currently obsessed with, whether it's a band or an artist or a writer or a filmmaker or whatever it may be, and I love that, and I can't imagine now living without that. Looking back on that time when all I had was this crappy fotonovela version of the Marx Brothers to go on, and nothing else to satisfy that desire, it's pitiable! But on the other hand, it was so exciting when something *did* come your way, when you stumbled on it, whether it was the thing you had heard about that you weren't even sure it really existed and there it was on the bookstore shelf or on the record rack, or running across somebody that turned out to know about it as well and also to be into it, and you just would chance on this person. It was so hard to make connections that when you did it was much more exciting, and you had a sense of a kind of quest being fulfilled. I don't think kids now really know what that's like at all, and that does make me feel a little bit sorry for them, because in the times before ABE Books and Amazon, if there was a particular book or issue of a magazine you were looking for, you might look for your whole life, and then every so often you had these discoveries that gave you hope and faith that it was worth the quest, because it could be done. And now you enter the name in

Google, and five minutes later it's on its way, overnight UPS, coming to your house. And that is both a wonderful thing and a sad thing, too.

Costello: I remember as a kid discovering and getting really into the comic *ElfQuest* only because some friends of my parents rescued them from the garbage somewhere because they knew I liked comics. I would never have heard of them if someone hadn't pulled them out of a trash can.

Chabon: I remember those, too. That's a good example of something there was really no way of obtaining information about, it would be this thing that would be available in some stores you would go to, and in others it would not, and you didn't know anything about who the people were who were making it, or how many of them there were, or how long it had been coming out for. There was no way of knowing. It was a realm of mystery.

Costello: What do you make, then, of how certain territories that used to be a part of this "realm of mystery" have become so integral to mainstream culture? Comic book characters like Iron Man and now even Rocket Raccoon, for instance, have suddenly become so central to contemporary popular culture on a scale we couldn't possibly have anticipated in the 1970s or 1980s.

Chabon: It's a very funny time to be a lover of all that stuff. I have this kind of thrilling ambivalence about the whole thing. One of the core experiences that I remember from my childhood is having fallen in love with this book of Greek myths by the D'Aulaires. I wrote an introduction to their Norse myths, but they also did a book of Greek myths that's very well known. I checked it out of my school library when I was in second grade and just devoured it, completely fell in love with it and felt that it was *mine*. And I remember one time walking through the—it wasn't actually called a library in my school in Columbia, Maryland, in 1970, it was called a media center— and I saw the D'Aulaires' Greek Myths book lying out on a table, implying that somebody else had been reading it. And I remembered that I was horrified by that! I grabbed it and I immediately returned it to its proper location on the shelf—I suppose if I was really hardcore I would have put it in the wrong place. But I put it back because I didn't like feeling that other people knew about this wonderful, secret mystery. And there's a little bit of that, or even a fair amount of that, in my experience right now as a fan of superheroes, particularly if you're talking about, say, Marvel Comics. My family and I have been watching *Marvel's Agents of SHIELD*. Toward the last third of the season they introduced the character of Deathlok the Demolisher, who is this completely obscure, not entirely forgotten, but never successful character that I loved as a kid—and here he is on network television in a fairly reasonable incarnation!

But at least I feel now, for the first time, that a lot of this stuff that's being done—whether it's the Star Trek films, especially the first one, or the Marvel movies, and to a greater or lesser extent things like the Guillermo del Toro Hellboy movies—is being created, almost from the very top down to the level of the cast, by people who love the material. I was watching a promo for the upcoming Marvel movies and the head of Marvel pictures is clearly a complete Marvel fan, a deeply knowledgeable fan, who loves this material. You get the sense from him and from Joss Whedon and some of the other people involved in these that they recognize the inherent value and worth of this material. Obviously these are massive corporations licensing and merchandising these huge interlocking sets of brands and trademarks and intellectual property. I recognize all that, and that actually does mess things up to one degree or another, but at least the material is sort of being lovingly and tenderly curated by people who truly understand that the comics themselves had value and continue to have value, and there's something more to it than, I don't know, trying to maximize the number of licensable properties. And let it be said, that was always a part of it back then, too, when I was a kid. It wasn't like it was this pure, sacred entity. It was cheap lunchboxes and lousy toys and cheesy record albums and all that kind of stuff. That was always a part of it. I'm comfortable with that. What's disheartening is seeing something private and beautiful and secret that you care about in the realm of pop culture exposed to the light in a way that's embarrassing and horrible. That's what's really painful. I don't want to name names but there have been numerous examples.

Costello: I just saw *X-Men: Days of Future Past* last weekend. I guess the *Avengers* movie did this, too, but I was impressed by how fully it embraced this sort of convoluted storytelling that was even less in the mold of the original Claremont/Byrne story and more like of a crazy crossover that ran through several annuals in 1992 or something. It didn't seem embarrassed of the sort of bigness of the universe and the strangeness of the characters and even the clunkiness of the plot devices—it just asks you to buy it all and enjoy it.

Chabon: And just come along! I think there was a mistake in aiming at what was believed to be the fan, or the fanboy, and what that was believed to mean, at a certain point in the not-so-distant past—lots of violence, lots of things blowing up, cool special effects, scantily clad female characters.

You know, all those things are really important, too [*laughter*], but there's so much more to what being a fan means. Part of what it has always meant is to be willing and able to engage with complicated material that gets really convoluted and intricate and has all kinds of nuances and shadings—how many different flavors of Kryptonite there are or how many versions of Earth there are in DC comics or in Marvel comics. You want to keep track of that stuff if you're a fan. It's important to you; it's a badge of your fanship. I think that is finally being recognized, and it's being done skillfully enough by professional screenwriters and directors that a general, less informed audience can come along for the ride.

Guardians of the Galaxy is going to be an interesting test. That is deeply quirky material with its roots in the period where the most prominent, most creative, most vital, most important, Marvel creators were all routinely dropping acid and smoking lots of marijuana. That's where all that material is rooted, whether it's the Guardians of the Galaxy or Warlock—or Rocket Raccoon, who begins in this insane, bizarre fantasia of Bill Mantlo's. That material is just *weird*, and it's going to be interesting how true they are to that weirdness—and if they are true to it, how well it goes over.

Costello: That's the strange effect of the success of the movies. It's almost as though the public will accept that these are characters they should care about *because* there is a movie about them. The grousing might be coming from within the comics fan community—"why are *these* guys getting a movie?" Just from my very unscientific survey of my students, they seem excited about it because it looks funny and they've gotten attached to the Marvel brand.

Chabon: There's a trust now. When you see that [Marvel logo] up front, you're like OK, I can relax, there's going to be a certain minimum quality.

Costello: I just got done teaching a 1980s comics class, including some superhero material. The students who were most knowledgeable about, or protective of, the continuity or the characters were not necessarily the stereotypical fanboys. In many cases it was young women who were really invested in X-Men history who would want to talk about how the story we were reading fit in, or whether it didn't, or how it got revised later on. Whenever I teach comics classes, there are always a few students who are really fannish, usually in a positive sense and sometimes in a negative sense, but they don't always fit the traditional profile.

Chabon: That was an important discovery of Chris Claremont in *X-Men*—

that if you handled the material in a certain way where you have a—the term "soap opera" is definitely meant to be disparaging—but you have a serialized plot focusing on the emotional and romantic lives of your characters while continuing to provide all the other things you're supposed to be providing, that you can really widen the traditional definition of fandom to include a lot of female readers who are just out there waiting to be acknowledged and recognized. And I think that's happening with these movies to a degree. I have two daughters and they were talking about it with each other and I just happened to be listening—they like Black Widow, they think she's awesome, but she's kinda *it* in terms of film. They're excited that she might get her own movie, but then they start thinking, "Who else would we like to see?" They don't like Wonder Woman, they don't want to see a whole movie about the Wasp. It's tough. Did you see all this this flack about She-Hulk?

Costello: I did—[*The Dark Knight Rises* and *Man of Steel* screenwriter] David S. Goyer said she was a green porn star for the Hulk to have sex with.
Chabon: What I liked about it, and what surprised me, was the strength of female support for that character, which I was unaware of. She was sort of after my time, and I never paid that much attention to her and didn't really know who was into She-Hulk, so I was surprised and pleased to discover what a popular character she appears to be with Marvel female readers.

It's very fun to talk about. It's reminding me that I always have this fantasy as I stand in the airport bookstore, looking at the magazines and wishing that there was a magazine that was on the level of the *New Yorker* or the *Atlantic* or *Harper's*, or maybe even a slightly higher level, that was about popular culture and music and movies, where you could discuss them on some level higher than *Entertainment Weekly* or a gaming magazine or a *Wizard* or whatever. Almost like a *Believer* magazine devoted to pop culture.

Costello: To come back to that idea of popular culture and comics as a realm of mystery, could you talk about making the transition to being on the other side of making a comic, the actual labor of writing the script for a comic book? Having grown up with them as a reader, having the experience as a child where comics are these things that just sort of appear and you don't necessarily know how they're made—what is process of writing a comic like for you?
Chabon: It's really hard [*laughter*]. I love doing it, I loved learning how to do it. It was partly trial and error and partly getting advice from my editor

at the time, Diana Schutz at Dark Horse, and looking at scripts I found for comics on the Internet, and having Diana send me scripts by writers she had worked with just to see how the format works. It's not nearly as standardized as screenplay writing. Different writers tend to have very idiosyncratic approaches to writing scripts, and they also often take into account their knowledge of the artist that they're working with, and how much or how little that artist likes to have written down on the page. There didn't seem to be one right way of doing it, and that interested me. But then, as I got into it, although I had studied comics and read theories of comics from Will Eisner and Scott McCloud and I knew about the importance of the word balloon text and the caption text, and how the action in the panel is shown and the interrelationship with what's *not* shown happening in-between panels . . . I knew the theory of it, but then to actually sit down and try to work with those fundamentals was a very novel experience, and really not at all like trying to write a screenplay, which I thought it was going to be somewhat like. In a way it's much richer. The screenplay environment on the page is a very impoverished environment. It's like the tundra or something, there's this grass and some buffalo moving around, and that's about it. With a screenplay you've just got description and dialogue, and you've got to keep your description really brief, and you have to keep your dialogue short, and you're working within these page constraints. With comics you can be as verbose as you want to because it's all going to get translated into ink on the page, pencil lines on the page. So you could be verbose, you could go overboard, you could be terse—that didn't matter. But also, you have more tools in your toolbox—you have describing what's happening in the panel, what we see, versus what we're *told* we're seeing, versus what the characters are *saying* is happening, and all three of those elements can be in complete disagreement with each other, which is a wonderful thing when that happens—that's three levels of irony that are possible. I liked getting the sense of that, the feel of how different and how rich it was. That was a really pleasurable feeling. Maybe I'd get faster if I did it more frequently, but I'm very slow and very laborious, and, you know, it doesn't pay very well, so I haven't been able to rationalize keeping it up, even though I did enjoy it.

Index